Cyber Smut

A collection of short stories & poetry

Edited by Julianne Ingles

guts publishing

For the smut lovers.

SMUT

noun

/smʌt/

1. [uncountable] *(informal)* stories, pictures or comments about sex that deal with it in a way that some people find offensive
    - *He can entertain audiences without resorting to smut.*
2. [uncountable, countable] dirt, ash, etc. that causes a black mark on something; a black mark made by this
    - *His face was covered with smuts from the engine.*

— Oxford English Dictionary

CONTENTS

EDITOR'S NOTE

It seemed to me that *Stories About Penises* would be a hard act to follow. To be honest, it wasn't so easy to let go of either. It was our first publication, and I suppose what you could call *my baby*. When I was discussing the anthology with one of the contributors she said, "Really what it's about is intimacy. You should do one about all those crazy mishaps on Tinder and Grindr." And that's where the idea came from. Yet, how does one encapsulate such an idea in a title? I came up with *Cyber Lives* and posted a call for submissions. But every time I read that title it was like some horrible flat note on an out-of-tune piano.

Shortly after I posted the call for submissions, I changed the title to *Cyber Smut*. It just flowed out so nicely, rolled off the tongue in such a way I could not resist. And it seemed to summarize, aptly, what I was trying to get at. All that shit that happens online. And with technology. Not only Tinder and Grindr, but everything. It seemed just perfect. Except when I googled Cyber Smut and Google told me this phrase was commonly used to describe porn. And I thought, fuck it, I don't care what Google says. It works. Somehow I knew that with the right image on the cover we could redefine this phrase. And push the boundaries of the literary anthology. And have a smashing collection of work.

Which is exactly what *Cyber Smut* is. A smashing collection of fiction, nonfiction and poetry—twenty-five pieces in total. Many address this issue of intimacy that I hoped to get at. Many deal with social media. Some just technology. The funny thing is that the majority of the work isn't all that smutty—I mean there is sex, plenty of it, or allusions to sex, but to be honest that is not the primary focus of this anthology. It is about loneliness and disconnection. It is about struggles with existential feelings. It is about the desire for fame, and an underlying desire to be heard and loved. It is about addiction and alienation and artificial intelligence. It is about the struggle with the 'unreal' world online and the desire to connect with the 'real' physical world. In short, it is about how technology has impacted our lives. Smuttily and otherwise.

My sincere thanks to all of our contributors. Your stories and poems have moved me, made me cry, made me laugh, and most of all made me think. About this insane world we live in and how we are all coping. I couldn't imagine publishing anything else in this anthology.

Many thanks to Gery Galabova, Corinne Jean-Jacques, Sao Pain and Charlie Mars—our readers who sifted through mounds of *Cyber Smut* submissions, read for hours and hours, and helped to select the work in this anthology. As well, an enormous thank you to Goldsmiths College for their ongoing support.

The biggest thank you of all goes to you! Thank you for purchasing this book and supporting Guts Publishing.

I hope you enjoy reading these stories and poems as much as I have. On the Contents page each title is labeled as (*f*) fiction, (*nf*) nonfiction, and (*p*) poem.

As always, stay well.

Julianne Ingles
6 July 2020

Cyber Smut

(take a deep breath, here we go)

JULIAN BISHOP
Tracker

You join the dots to track my dashes,
my nine to five daily routine captured
by your app—each lap of routine timed

to the second, assigned to a precise location,
each deviation, coffee stop unfolding
on an online map. You log me in spots

flashing across a screen, my lifelines traced
in the palm of your hands, homing in
on stops to form fresh lines of inquiry:

who were you talking to outside Boots?
why did you zig-zag and not go straight?
Oh spy who loves but doesn't trust me

you programmed my phone into a drone
that circles me 24/7—you may have reason:
peace of mind for the family circle

reassures the blurb on Ispyoo, as the loops
bubble-wrap your screen, a pattern of ties
that tighten around me like a noose.

KRISTAN X
Metrics

When she joins Twitter you are her first follower. Before she has a profile picture. Before she has a bio. She's an egg, blank and new, zero, zero, zero. And you are her first.

Within a week, however, she has twice as many followers as you. It's as if Twitter is something she's been waiting for all her life. Something which has been waiting for her. She's never not on it. Updates her feed a hundred, two hundred times per day. As natural and as regular to her as breathing.

One month in, she has a hundred times your following. They shower her with hearts and retweets. She posts a picture of herself first thing in the morning—another before she goes to bed. She posts pictures of you as well: your big hand enveloping hers. A selfie of you kissing.

"They like you," she says. When she says *they* she is talking about her followers. An army of benign, invisible fans. "They think you're good for me."

You realise very quickly that she tells them everything. After fucking you lie tangled together in bedsheets. She fetches her phone from the bedside table and taps out an update. Tells them she came. Describes to them the exquisite ache she feels in the minutes afterwards. Tells them (just as she has often told you) how much she loves the feeling of spooning with you, your arm across her chest.

She kisses you, long and slow on the lips. It's only after she pulls back that you notice she's holding her phone. That the camera is rolling.

Her followers are like a pet. A part of her. An inquisitive, gently burbling army that surrounds her always. She asks you questions on their behalf. "Have you ever been skinny dipping?" she asks. Or, "Will you get another tattoo?" She plucks these questions from the air, like a seer consulting gods. You answer. She dutifully taps out your response.

She hits a million followers. One million. Three times the population of the city in which you live. More people than you will meet in a year. More people than you will know in your lifetime. Every now and then she is recognised in the street: people wave, or cheer, or call her name. She blushes with pleasure every time this happens.

You make your own Twitter profile private without really thinking about it. Within an hour she's at your flat, arriving like a storm. She is furious. "It's a waste," she says. "A complete waste." She stabs the screen of her phone. Think, she implores you, of how many followers you could have. And you wouldn't even have to post anything. Wouldn't have to *do* a damn thing. You'd get them just from being with her.

She bristles. Her followers (over a million of them now) bristle too. Your phone shivers constantly on the surface of your desk and you don't attend to it. She sees you not attending to it, and looks at you wounded. She throws herself onto your bed and lies curled up on her side, phone out, her face bluelit. "You should tell them something," she says. "An explanation at least. You owe them that."

"I don't owe *them* anything," you say. She snorts. Taps the screen in a rapid, angry staccato.

Later you fuck, roughly and at length. You think that it might be the last time. She bites your arm and you pull her hair, driving into her. She grunts, almost like a sob. Afterwards she sits on the end of your bed facing the mirror on your wardrobe. Musses her hair a little further. Smears her makeup with one finger, then takes a picture.

The argument is forgotten, but she's distant after that. Her followers take up more and more of her time. She's left her job. "Sorry," she says, whenever you are together. "Sorry, sorry, just one minute." She doesn't want to leave them waiting, she explains. One minute and then she'll be with you. She taps frantically, then slips the phone away into her bag. It buzzes in the dark like a trapped animal.

She has two million followers. The number is growing faster now. Crazily, recklessly fast. She'll hit three million within a month. The speed with which that number changes makes you feel faintly sick. Vertiginous. As though the ground is dropping away from beneath your feet.

She wears brand new clothes each day now. She smells different. You do not fuck anymore, but she cuddles with you in her bed while she replies to messages. Kisses you for the camera. Requests, on one occasion, that you give her a love bite in the crook of her neck. It takes two tries before she is satisfied. If you fall asleep she is gone by the time you wake.

You have an argument. A brief, violent, stupid one. It comes from nothing, and it absorbs everything. "You're jealous," she says. "This is the best thing that has ever happened to me and you can't just be happy for me. You have to ruin it, don't you?"

There are many things you want to say. All of them sound, in your head, childish and simplistic and dumbly jealous. You say them anyway. She has her phone in her hand and as you say these things you can sense the weight of three million ghosts in the air around her, packing the room so dense there isn't air, so full of breathing watching needing bodies that you can't see her anymore, that you don't know who you're talking to.

She tells you to leave. She's crying. You do and it is windy outside. The air as heavy as it gets before a storm. You walk at random until the fire in your gut dies down. You call an Uber. As you're waiting outside a corner shop a middle-aged man with baggy eyes lurches up to you and grabs your forearm. "You broke her heart, you asshole. Asshole." He releases you. He's gone.

The back of your Uber is warm and dim. The driver eyes you in the mirror. "I always thought you were bad for her," he says. You tell him to stop the car and let you out there. You'll walk the rest of the way. Which you do, but a group of teenage girls follows you, whispering behind their hands. *Is it him? It's him. It's definitely him.* Outside your apartment door a skinny boy rife with piercings spits on the ground at your feet.

You get inside. You lock the door. You turn off your computer. You turn off your phone. Your apartment is dark and quiet. Nothing buzzing or blipping or humming as it charges. The view from your window looks out across the city. Night is falling. Her ghosts are out there, stalking the streets. The ground is falling away beneath your feet.

You draw the curtains. You lie down in the dark and wait. In your head you are repeating it over and over again. *You don't owe them anything. You don't owe them anything.*

LYDIA HOUNAT
closure, decoded

</

how you knew to wash blood out of things,
<cold water>, <quick>,
        the moments I hated you:
                coffee-sweat mood
        the moments I adored you:
                soaked lentils stewed

<meta name= "colour: 'furious'/>
remedy: try to tell you / with my teeth stinging
I won't swing the beach; clog my hair; steam your chest;
sink into your arm
repeat function: remedy:
        I'm not saying <I will miss you>
        I'm saying   !error missing file!

You will be missing
        though you were a word glittering on my tongue
        missing like a strand or a feather / plucked / malware
<body><script> type= "{[{'the misplaced smells I will have
to burn now'}, {'the bloodshot negatives and your
                sweater too small to fit'}, {'mould-stuffed
screensaver'},
{corrupted fruit hard drives}, {the rind of your monitor
troubleshooting my underwear},

{'cremate River Tamar'}, {'chase and check'}, {this html never made sense}, {a connection failure}]}". />.

(intensity)

PIOTR BOCKOWSKI
a sister of her sister. (No… it can't be her!)

Loops of internalised circulation. Tunnels tangled for thousands of miles overlapping. Twin sister was sent in an electric capsule, moving through the vast strains of the mycelium that undergrows the jungle. Enclosed in a solid sphere, like a spore. With her glance teasing a stiffening pipe of an air conditioning exhaust. There was fungi discharge dripping from it.

Tubular cracks of vehicle surrounded her with a subtle web, overwhelming with an unexpected but persistent migraine. Recalling traces of mold on the wall, pain was triggering the superflat strains of her nerves. Disturbing intensity of light. Poking edges. Smell, like a severe hallucination, grew to monstrous dimensions of an utterly frightening childhood memory, constantly changing its form. Each time revealing an even more hideous nature of herself. Recalling forgotten weirdness. The dead sister brought to the shack slums in the desert of the night. Watching a non-existent movie through her body, like a dream device. Deliric archaeology of the immediate past. Fights of beastie sisters in a cage. She tried to masturbate to expel this mirage, in an attempt to desperately shake it off her temples, but the bodkin of orgasmic contraction paralyzed her face muscles with bitter numbness. Her mouth filled with a taste of fungi. She collapsed awaiting. In the very depth of the jungle, the capsule stopped.

The central concentration was located directly below corpuscular silos of nano-maternity. Swallowed by a half-extinct volcano, an atomic rector was receiving emissions from all sorts of different parts of monster island, accumulating them into a critical mass. The reactor was a melting pot for twin sister mutations, creating a gigantic cocoon of a techno-womb trapped within an obscene mouth of an electromagnetic chimney. The twin sisters' swarm gathered in the bottom apex of a concavity, connected together through smart devices of virtual penises, radiating digital sperm. Huge beyond the twin's perception, the nano-maternity reactor constituted her event horizon. She felt as if she were in a completely open empty space, in the forgotten pout of the ocean. On a freak atoll.

The twin sisters' laboratory is a blend of institutional rot and medicalized breed, clotted with fungi. Ocean digested by a c.anal. Jungle closes in on both sides. Here is the place where twin sisters are transplanted. Notion of monstrous biotech laboratory environment, as a total ontological category, encapsulating the realm of all twin sisters. Concrete layering of the experimentation chambers becomes an immediate extension of brain wiring, enclosing itself within it and projecting it at the same time. Being an ultimate construct of the jungle immunology system, spheral urban cocoon, that materialises its project within high-tech presence. Virtual communication, which enfolds the (hyper)natural dimension of the laboratory, functions instead of her neuronal system. New online applications for portable electronic testicles have automatically replaced some parts of her brain.

Her migraine started dissolving with the first ejaculation of digital sperm. All of the sisters were spraying it around them, filling the techno-womb with an intricate network of artificial gene transfers. Digital sperm was the only valid virtual currency in the electric jungle, stimulating awkward sex implosions of neofungus.

The digital sperm of several different twin sisters was mixing inside a brain scanner. Their virtual penises plugged into its interface. They were playing a multidimensional quantum game inside it, making points by outlining spheres of genetic influence. Appropriating the proximity to one another, taking over each other's fields of influence. Pinpoint alternative possibilities of neural targets. The brain scanner was able to model a new twin cocoon based on the chimerical patchwork of juxtaposed DNA. It could also print a variety of cellular patterns and all of it simulated by her new generation virtual penis.

Twin sister looked around. The space was fragmented by a cluster of holographic domes, enclosing crowds of sisters, crawling on each other like insects. Hypnotised by the trance of revolting chemistry. She was getting gradually enraged beyond comprehension, instinctively imagining a severe and methodical procedure of segregating sisters into enclosed vacuum cocoons. Based on the types of deformity they have worn around their slit eyes, the group units were defined by a certain category. Think about any whimsical way of exterminating her twins. Useless critters, blindly gather together, just to eat each other's dirt, smearing it on the rim of their orifices. To breed more of themselves alike. Swollen in a cocoon. Swallowing slime. "What an utter waste of space," she muttered, detested. An enormous crack opened inside her.

Progeny of beyond. As curious as suspicious. Heroes of her own paranoia. Losers of her common sense. Lunatic twins.

She was hiding something in her hair. An enormous tangle, she picked a few lost threads stuck to dust structures, carrying radiating particles and mutating spores. She searched within her, entering the hair-brain abyss of magnificent volume. Gentle strokes of her fingers irritated a scab-colony of suppurating glands that were discharging thick liquid tissue, made out of the collective existence of her clones. Miniature embryo viruses were coming from perfectly voided nihilism of technological death. Re-enacting fantasy variants of possible creatures, with their ridiculous squeaks and amoeboid body projections. Round or oblong organ displacement. Yet to be.

Was this strange body worm coming from inside her brain? Feeding on her hair. She will keep creeping back in. The sister in question. Looking somehow insectile.

Now for her. Creeping in the back of her head, she has never quite suppressed the feeling that she is not herself exactly but rather some-body else. Movement in a crowd of random twin sisters brought a discovery of paradoxical detachment. Surrounded by morphing headpieces, she tried to reach them desperately but unsuccessfully. Frozen in a corrupted sequence of animation. The heads simply couldn't turn around. A confusingly smeared angle in a multi-exposition tumour apparatus. It wasn't possible to see her twin sisters' faces. They were non-existent, covered with layers of glitchy masks and distorted landscapes, their fake depth perspective. The imploding surface of pits, swallowing swollen tentacles, was powered by a pattern of microscopic injections. Countless semi-organic tubes were growing inside their hair and delivering nano-twins that way. Nano-twins extracted from the most potent mutagenic sisters directly into fungi spores. She sucked on the pits a great deal. A sweaty ball of hair made her choke.

She seemed half-hairbrained. But she didn't want to drink her hair now. "You are too foul to live!" said her sister. "Why are you not killed for your horrible shapes?" She need not have said this, her eyes betraying her intentions all too clearly. And there she was. A middle-sex twin emerged from the gene pool. At the edge of the jungle. Albino freak. Self-hypnotised to perform auto-cannibalism. Staring at her own tail's movement. Coldly supervising the coil snaking behind her back. Twisting the spine with an empty look. Frozen awe.

Stricken by this encounter, she finally realised that the sister had a sister who wasn't her, but lived in her body. Who was she? Her twin, hiding inside her. Was she spying on her all this time? Certainly, but not just by herself. All of them were following each other's gestures. The integrity of her self has been forever compromised. Her brain seemed to rattle against the sides of her skull. She hissed: "You monstrous thing, how I despise you!" She knew that she hadn't been like that before.

Certainly she wasn't like that before. Not as confused. Her body has never fought itself with such desperation. And now, her immunology system got into some sort of realization, confronting itself as an essentially fragmented entity of different genotypes, contrasting microbiological mechanisms, not functioning together but despite one another. This new system dynamic seemed to her as fascinating as frightening. She toyed with the idea of her inner organs being at war, especially the nervous circuit, which didn't seem so actual anymore. Separate segments of the spine eating each other's tails and all together raping the brain. Limbic gland biting into the cortex. Left side of the brain constantly torturing the right side, while at the same time the other one was infecting her with an unknown virus, beyond words… They run the body as a racist organ farm, with their very own sex slaves of limbs and pits, moist with completely different discharge. Biotech madness within her-any-self. Her just-revealed hybrid nature must have been of fungal origin, there was no doubt about it. Or should she rather say—them? For fungi are many within the same mycelium, mapping the jungle with their tropical extensions, they are creating a virtual model for the future twin sister breeding ground. So, these twins were living already inside her own body, which she has never really owned. She was a portable organic laboratory whore, where experiments of the new genetic mutations were cruelly confronting their freaky effects at her expense. She looked at herself in the reflection of the c.anal surface—oh, how random was her look! Being just but an extension of her biotech laboratory, that created her brain cocoon in the depths of its techno-womb. Prefabricated cynically in the sewer. Feeling betrayed by monster island.

She was roaming through the jungle, in circles. She couldn't stand herself. Why were twin sisters always so alone in the jungle? Why was the fungi laboratory breeding exclusively female mutants? What's the purpose of this insect-ish feel to the experiments on monster island? Inner organs murmur. Flesh's flash! Melancholic whisper of orifices, breathing. These and similar questions were echoing in her womb, unknowing that the very womb was the most direct answer for them. Her womb itself was the essential mutation device, involved with genetic chimeras, recreating its own bio-molecular environment anew. Pregnant with perverse research of the neofungus laboratory. Chewing the fertility of trash.

The synthetic trash island, eaten by fungi, creates a new environment of infection. If she hadn't been infected, she wouldn't have had to mutate. The infection—like any other art—is a domain of potentiality. Quite so. Infected, she has turned polymorphous perverse. Followed by her hidden twin sister, who enveloped herself in the jungle. Watching her without being noticed? Thus, those who employ secret agencies must monitor them! The agent knows who she is spying on, but she never knows who is spying on her. She snaked her limb around the body. Wrapped it around as strong and as supple as a tropical vine. She will just cave in. She will. Or maybe she won't. Because she doesn't like the idea already. Finding herself lost in the jungle. She did about everything to find her twin sister. Looking in all directions at once, blindly. Has anybody seen her? Downward spiral of the spine. All the way to twin sister's second brain. What was her excuse for the endless non-sequiturs? Now, she needs a large piece of sleep again. Or maybe it's just an urge to take a nano-twin pill? Monster island is questioning itself more than ever this time. Let's mystify the illusion of a weather forecast. Across the wasteland.

Across the ocean in no time. The wasteland is not inside the island's jungle anymore, but the isle on the wasteland. Floating. The ocean is the wasteland itself. Floating fungi, shining like an eye and growing on water. It glistened darkly in its intricate patterns. Liquid morel? Melting knobs of void. An edge of the vortex, on every horizon of the trash archipelago, was composed exactly like her bizarre eye deformation that her twin sister has tried to imitate with digital make-up. Made out of theoretical fungi, it resembled sign language of microbes. Internet false feet. The desperate struggle of a unicellular organism to duplicate.

23

(get a glass of wine please)

(Feeling better now? Yeah, P Bockowski, totally intense)

(now stretch your smutty imagination)

LYDIA LUKE
copper & lead

one

Jeremiah's a *good* man.

we met when i moved down to Birmingham to study
at the polytechnic. i was living with Joyce, who i'd met
in my first few months there. she hadn't been in England
a year but already had a heap of friends & dragged me to
a different house party every weekend.

i noticed him in the corner as soon as we walked in.
hands in his pockets, locs packed into a cap.

he stood alone most of the night.
not waiting on nothing or no-one;
looking steadfast & sturdy.
then the DJ played *Natty Dread*
& it was as if the bassline was built
into his neck. it travelled down his
spine, bounced within his knees.
he was a moving statue at one with the speaker.

i was mesmerised.
i couldn't keep my
attention off him.

he had these eyes —
springs that kept flowing.
like the Atlantic Ocean, but without the grief.
with him there'd be nowhere to put my feet.

i would just drift 'til i was weightless.
you'd think that dangerous but i felt safe.
most men like him aren't safe.
they're free. they lie, they drink.
they hate things to stop hating themselves.
but his eyes, his look, felt safe.

i was watching with such abandon,
i didn't notice he was watching me back.
right then i knew we'd marry.
and we did;
ten months later.

two

we moved into a little house, with yellow walls. Jeremiah
got a job as a factory worker
at the Longbridge Plant.
i worked part-time at Birmingham Library.
Agnes & Derek were born soon after.
we went to the park every Sunday,
took them to the seaside when we could.
Jeremiah would run around with them all day
and tell them stories at night. though our lives were
small, we felt so big & watched over.

my husband wanted to take me
& the children to Ghana.
he thought we should see
our motherland.

"we can't afford that kind of trip
darling. and what's the need?
it's not like you've been to Jamaica
& i was born in Sheffield."

tutting & rolling his eyes, he picked
me up in his arms.

"you can't fight me Miss Nancy;
my Ghanaian princess.
we're gonna go."

he kissed the borders of my face.

"we're gonna go,
we're gonna go."

he always explored me; finding
a new way to unlock my dress or jeans.
i'd wrap my legs tight around him, holding onto
his shoulders 'til flowers fell from my mouth.

the neighbours didn't think a poor couple
with children should make such a noise;
but we didn't care,
& we always did.
we loved in high tides.

three

a medical company visited Longbridge.
they were looking for volunteers to take part
in a clinical experiment for a steroid that 'increased
performance' & 'enhanced productivity'.

"Nancy, dem offer me £150 to swallow
tablet & take mi blood? i'd be a dunce man
not to do it. and with all the night shifts i've
been doing the past few months, i'll be able

to tek you & di pickney dem to Ghana before
Agnes start school."

i was reticent, which upset him.
he couldn't understand why i wasn't
excited to receive such a blessing.
but a feeling; this thing inside me,
wondered what was making my measured man
so wildly optimistic. so blindly trusting.
was it love? opportunity? or a chance to escape?
i didn't know which frightened me more.

i came home to an envelope of money with a note:

we're gonna go, we're gonna go, we're gonna go
took a fiver for the pub
love you x

four

a letter from the company came two weeks later.
we sat at opposite sides of the kitchen table,
not quite knowing what was on the other's face.

dear Mr Macintosh,

thank you for participating in the clinical experiment.

based on your test results, your blood composition
contains 25% lead and 25% copper. we don't know the
full extent of the side effects, but we can confirm your
muscle tissue will mutate also.

since it is a reaction to our steroid, we will supply you
with the medication needed to keep you stable. you'll

collect it weekly from your place of employment.

*do not attempt to sue or speak to the newspapers. you
will be cut off your medication if you do so & your
contract with your employer will be terminated
immediately.*

we do sincerely apologise for any harm caused.

it shook in Jeremiah hands, the words hovering
over us like blackbirds wanting to take flight.

five

"course the pickney dem can stay the night. you don't
even need fi ask me! you can sleep here too if unu want
to. my offer still stands."

Joyce paused to snuggle a sleeping Derek.

"i'm glad you're meeting with a housing officer.
me cyaan' understand how you're still living in that
soulless den wi dat Frankenstein man."

things had gradually gotten worse.
the blackbirds in that letter swarmed our
house & made home in every corner.

as his body mass became metal; he suffered from violent
headaches & was missing work, often three or four days
at a time. his wages were split in half to cover the cost of
importing his medication, so i had to take on work
cleaning houses to keep us afloat.

i got really sick & found out i'd contracted lead

poisoning in my womb. i recovered fine enough
but Jeremiah stopped coming to bed.
he stopped touching me, stopped kissing me.
his neck tilted away from me.
that bassline was now a sad song.
he wouldn't let me look at him like i used to.
he'd lock himself in the spare room;
staring at shadows on the butter-like walls.
mind muddied like boots in war.

"how you nuh lef him yet? he was the one chupid enough
to offer himself for some nonsense experiment. now
you're the one running yourself inna the ground, taking
on mammy work. 'cos 'im a poppy show. mi glad i never
marry no man. men bring you nuttin but pain &
frustration. i tell yu dem are all useless from birth. but
your man Nancy, your man a fool fi true!"

she drew on her cigarette & chuckled.

Agnes, with her father's long legs,
toppled onto the sofa & into my lap.

"mummy, Aunty Joyce says we're
moving into a new house. are we?"

i sighed & readjusted for my children.

"we might be"

"with a television & telephone
& radio like we used to have?"

Derek, with his father's eyes,
woke up in Joyce's arms & listened.

"perhaps Agnes"

"is Daddy coming too?"

both of my children watched me pensively.

"i'm not sure darling."

six

her office had no air.
that or it was at odds with me.
either way, the blackbirds from home
followed me there & perched on
my shoulder.

she did her buttons all the way up
& had short colourless nails.

"so, you're looking to be
placed into social housing?"

i nodded & i gave her my documents.
she scanned them briefly.

"says here you're legally married.
what's your husband's occupation?"

"he's a factory worker at Longbridge."

she sniffed & wiped her glasses,
her face filled with assumptions.

"unfortunately, Mrs Macintosh, because there's no

written proof you're being made homeless; you might be
put toward the bottom of the waiting list. but
you do have two children & are taking on extra work so
the council might be sympathetic to your situation."

she softened with vicious pity.

"i'm assuming your husband ran off.
the men at Longbridge have that tendency."

my heart moved. slowly
at first, then it raced thru my chest
like a tampered Ferrari. heavy with
those damned swarming blackbirds.

no.

she was wrong, Joyce was wrong
in how they spoke about him.
they didn't know him.
they didn't know the mountain i'd met
seven years ago, with the safe eyes.

no.

he's not a fool.
Jeremiah's a *good* man.

"will you excuse me?"

i walked out the office,
out the building, down the road.
speed found its way to my legs & i ran.

i ran & ran & ran.

like something was chasing me.
like i was being pulled by a rope.
i ran straight back to my house
where i knew my husband would still be.

seven

Jeremiah was in the shower.
he wouldn't when anyone was home.
said it was horrible to hear
but he sounded like a symphony;
rainfall on a tin roof.
i went up the stairs 'til i reached
the bathroom door.
it spoke & i opened it.

i watched him.

he got out the bathtub & grabbed
a towel, his back towards me.
it had no skin. his whole body
was a marble painting of
copper & lead.
water droplets competed to get down
to his waist & catch the light from the window.

i was mesmerised.
i couldn't keep my
attention off him.

exactly like how we met.

i was watching with such abandon,
i didn't notice he was watching me back.

with the force of a grieving wife,
i threw myself onto him.
he hoisted me up, tearing
at my tights & kissing me.
all over my face,
my neck, my shoulders;
like he used to.
he belonged to me again.
he was my moving statue.

we were back in our bed,
covered by walls & windows.
he sang long thick sonnets in me.
we drew breath as one being.
his lifeblood was
warm & tinny & *everywhere*.
my eyes rolled back from into black water.

(cy·ber /ˈsībər / adj - relating to or characteristic of the
culture of computers, information technology, and virtual
reality: *the cyber age*)

ROGER CRAIK
In the Machine (2004)

Asleep, his mind in the machine
switched off, he dreams of M. C. Escher's
slender mantis-earwig, swivel-eyed, poised
above his private messages and their
presumed and bold replies, its long
antennae twitching like slow whips.

Bolt-awake
he knows a vigorous splashing of the face
from palm-cupped hands dispels the fears.
Even so, eleven paces and he's
at his desk: thumb, the static-crackling hum, the screen
taking its time with things, the icons
forming like religion. . . and of course. . .
He could have told you this.

KES BROOKLAND
Document Recovery

Frustration into finger-clenching snapping
Pain, betrayed and abandoned in
Shiny chrome faces all around,
Language-scripts pooling and spinning in
Your head, document recovery, anger
Grows with infantile incoherency to
Policemen in the rain.
Decaying hail blurring stream-of-consciousness
Into ink-stains, lost data, blots of rising angry

Escape of amorphous body, space woven between
Thought and narrative, twanging chromatophore-bomb!
With eight eyes, eight limbs blinking
Invincible sidereal as deep blue sea (colourized)
Tears away to void of space (colourized), bring
Down furious spined tentacles and render ash
And raging nothing-sentences, of textual loops and circles
never stopping
Document recovery.
Document recovery.

CALUM WALKER
Purpose

A man wanders with purpose through a wasteland.

This is the only life he has ever known. He was born in desolation, though he is not sure why. He has seen rivers run with blood. He has seen his brothers and sisters die in senseless agony. He has seen flocks of birds plummet to the ground, dead, with no impetus beyond the collective loss of the will to live. He has seen the stars in the sky blink out of existence, one by one, until all that remained was the infinite blackness of the night's sky. What he hasn't seen much of is colours. His world is one of dark greys and browns, of gravel and mud, with only the crimson hue of blood or the amber glow of fire offering any respite. He has heard tales—tales of a world before this, one of promise and light and hope and laughter and life. And he has heard one tale in particular, the tale of a relic—a demi-god who has stood guard alone for millennia, protecting the knowledge of this ancient world, only offering it to a select few travellers fortuitous enough to make their way to the deity, so long as their hearts and ideals are pure.

And so the man wanders. He hopes that he wanders towards this deity, although he has no means of knowing if the path he walks is the right one. He hopes his heart is pure and his ideals are, too, although he has no means of knowing the deity's metric for this. He lies awake at night, wondering to himself whether he is worthy of the deity's gift of knowledge. He grimaces, as he mentally recounts in vivid detail all his sins. He questions if he is beyond redemption in the deity's eyes, although he attempts to pacify these thoughts as he remembers his acts of kindness and compassion. Perhaps they would be enough to counter his cruelties. It tears him apart that he has no way of knowing for sure. He cannot measure with objectivity the weight of his deeds as he can the water he scoops up in his flask, or the number of stones he needs to build shelter. He hopes he will be able to, someday.

* * *

Time immeasurable has passed. The man has grown older and his body frailer, but his drive burns stronger than ever. Any rational being would have surely yielded the fight to stay alive by now, letting death claim victory, but the man strides onward, will unbroken, for his travels are the only truth he has ever known.

At long last, in the far distance, beyond the sand and dust and smog, he sees it. A construct out of place, standing proud among the wreckage of a temple whose architecture is foreign to the man. He is in disbelief—this must be a mirage, surely? It would not be the first, after all. But his subconscious urges him forward, and he runs, faster than he has ever run, the sand and dust and smog whipping violently against his face, but he does not notice, for his senses are overwhelmed, fixated on the lone construct in the middle of the wasteland. And the man sees that it is real. He does not dare to touch it, for such an act would be blasphemy, but he knows in his heart and in his mind that he is staring at a being that is really, truly, tangibly there. He sees that the being sits atop an altar of wood. Its body is alien to the man—a pure rectangular shape, whose angles are sharper and more perfect than any he has seen before. He circles around it—from the back it protrudes a mass of tentacles, tentacles that seem to connect to some sort of monolith nestled beneath the altar. From the front it omits an overwhelming light, an ever-changing light of colours and images the man would never have been able to conceive

44

of himself. Their majesty makes him weep, weep harder than he has ever wept, harder than when he witnessed his brothers and sisters die, harder than when the flock of birds fell and perished, harder than when the very last star in the sky dimmed out of existence. He manages to compose himself, just about, with the subconscious reminder that he stands before a deity, a deity who is judging his every action, and that this act of sentimentalism would not reflect well on him or his ideals. He steels himself, and prepares to ask the deity the questions that have plagued his life since as long as he can remember.

"O Ancient One," he speaks, "I, a humble traveller, have come all this way to ask of you to impart your wisdom and knowledge of this world, and the one that came before it."

The deity speaks in a soothing voice, one without cadence or accent. "You do not possess administrator rights to access this feature."

The man is abashed. He kneels in reverence. "I humbly apologise, O Ancient One. I spoke to you as if we are equals, when I am but a speck of dust in your presence. I can only ask you find it in your heart to forgive me. I am willing to tend to your whims and needs no matter the cost, and in return, if you are willing to impart your wisdom and knowledge, I would be eternally in your favour."

The deity speaks again. "A fatal exception OE has occurred at 0028:C0034B23. The current application will be terminated."

The man is baffled by the deity's terminology, but once he parses it, he panics. "Please, O Ancient One! I have spoken out of line. There is no excusing my behaviour, I know it to be true. I shall do everything in my power to repent for my mistakes, from the mistake of my birth to the mistakes I have made addressing you. I carry the burden of my kin on my shoulders, my promises to them to discover the meaning of this world in which we live and suffer and die. I can only beg of you, from the bottom of my heart, not to terminate me, not while my quest remains incomplete. I can be of great service to you, O Ancient One. I swear it."

The deity does not respond. The man waits, his feeble heart pumping blood faster than it ever has before. He waits, knowing that death at the hands of the Ancient One may come at any moment, with no time for him to process the event.

"Your PC ran into a problem and needs to restart." The deity breaks the silence at last. "We're just collecting some error info, and then we'll restart for you."

The man sighs with relief. "You are a most gracious and forgiving deity. I do not know what I did to deserve such absolution, but I am forever in your debt. If only mortals were able to forgive so purely as you, perhaps this realm would be a kinder place to live... O, Ancient One, is this the wisdom you impart to me? That in this world of horror and cruelty and bloodshed, where only the strongest survive, that forgiveness is the path to prosperity? Yes, I can see it now, a world without conflict or hatred, just kindness, overwhelming kindness for my fellow man. I sought my answers in the ethereal, and now the ethereal has responded with the answer I should have realised decades ago. Yes, thank you, Ancient One, for your wisdom has proven invaluable to—"

"Your 30-day free trial period of WinRAR has ended," the deity suddenly declares. "Please click here to purchase the full version."

"Ancient One?" the man splutters. He feels his heart sink. "O Ancient One, please, you misunderstand. My travels have lasted far longer than a month. I have been seeking your guidance since I was but a mere child. I was born in desolation. I have seen rivers run with blood. I have seen my brothers and sisters die in senseless agony. I have seen flocks of birds plummet to the ground, dead, with no visible impetus other than a collective loss of the will to live. I have seen the stars in the sky blink out of existence, one by one, until all that remained was the infinite blackness of the night's sky. O, Ancient One, the suffering I have seen spans so, so much longer than a mere month. Every waking moment of my consciousness has been pain. And you seek to diminish that in favour of material gain? That is all that matters to you? That I purchase your knowledge?"

The deity says nought. Its light, once effervescent, now glows a harsh blue, and in that silent blue the man sits, and he contemplates.

"I understand now, Ancient One," the man says at last, "that yours is not the wisdom I seek. I shall forever value the mercy and compassion you so briefly showed me. From henceforth I shall share in that mercy and compassion with my fellow travellers, for that is the only reprieve from the darkness. That is what I choose to value from this encounter, but no more. Fare thee well."

With newfound resolve, the man continues his voyage. His destination has changed, but his determination remains the same. He leaves the deity, alone on its altar, with silence and ruin as its only companions, as once more a man wanders with purpose through a wasteland.

RADOSLAV ROCHALLYI
Biological mimicry

~~Programmed~~ behaviour

hiding ~~in their own decisions~~

Preferences ~~and Choices~~

~~long~~-**defined** ~~formulas~~

The ~~thoughtful self~~

<u>trimmed by a</u> fence ~~of conceit~~

about ~~free mind~~

~~and~~ **self**-~~importance.~~

(you're probably not real)

LIAM HOGAN
Plastic People

Christmas Eve and the Ghosts are fucking.

They hadn't been doing that when I crossed the square earlier. Heading for a festive dinner-for-one I'd pretty much tuned them out, despite the Santa hats and flashing reindeer antlers.

They're naked now though. Naked, and fucking. It's an eerie, silent orgy. Other than a couple of trios and one sprawling quintet, the Ghosts—or 'plastic people'—have paired off. Not always in a boy-girl arrangement, I notice as I brush through a pair of writhing women, the hologram fragmenting and reforming in my wake.

From the relative safety of a shop awning, away from the main projectors, I take a longer look. Their naked motions are scripted and overtly choreographed: porn-flick sex rather than actual screwing. The women look like they're enjoying it too much and the men not enough. The virtual bodies are implausibly proportioned and all far too beautiful.

Usually, plastic people are mere seat-holders in restaurants; designed to give you the illusion the place is busy as you glance through the window, vacating their place as flesh and blood punters arrive to take the tables. Or they're ghostly pedestrians strolling across empty squares and boulevards to discourage the sort of antisocial behaviour that prefers to go unobserved.

That such witnesses are fake is by the by; it is the sense of being watched that the town planners were aiming for, something the ever-present CCTV hasn't generated for years.

The Ghosts might have been decommissioned once the novelty faded, had some bright spark not turned them into walking adverts for the clothing outlets, defraying their running costs, their outfits changing with the seasons, sometimes with the weather.

Even so, for all but the most fashion-conscious they've become mere wallpaper. It's only on the odd occasions when they're programmed to do something different from the pedestrians they crudely mimic that you notice them at all.

An orgy certainly meets that criteria. I wonder that no-one has done it before.

I raise my phone, tap the augmented reality button and aim it at the closest couple; but all I get from the hidden AR code is a dropdown menu for next year's spring fashions, clothes they're very much not wearing. No artists' or hackers' tags; not even an advert for a Kings Cross Porn Emporium. Probably the work of some bored teenager with too much time and bandwidth on his hands. A talented amateur.

And then the nearest guy stops sucking the cock of his virtual partner, half-turns towards me, and *winks*.

That gets my attention, especially as it's my own rather shocked looking face he uses to wink with.

An arm snakes through mine and a soft voice at my side asks: "So, what do you think?"

I want to look down, to the pressure at my hip, to see whether it's the double prongs of a contraband Taser or the airjet needle of a date-rape hypo, the playthings of a disreputable bunch of anarchist pranksters that had once plagued the Square Mile, but I don't. I daren't, for fear that's the sort of action that might trigger its use. I glance sideways instead, catch the girl's profile as she watches the jerking forms before us. She doesn't look much like an eco-rebel, or data-mugger, or worse. And there's no earpiece visible behind her shoulder-length chestnut hair. She's here to listen, not to watch.

I'm being tested.

"I'm flattered," I say, and the edge of her lip quirks up.

"Don't be," she says, "it's not just for your benefit."

I peer slowly round. A sleigh ho-ho-ho's by, a bare-chested Santa being pleasured by two pendulous breasted elves, and a woman scurries past, her hands clapped over the eyes of her equal-height son. A son who, no doubt, already has his own pair of unlogged and unverified virtual reality goggles stashed away at the back of his sock drawer and is accustomed to watching far worse than the tame action playing out here.

But then, mother knows all about *that*. The hands over the eyes are so that they can both still pretend to ignore the trio of elephants in the room; the teenage son's rampant hormones, the cheap and easy availability of high quality porn, and the fact that for him to be there at all his mother must have had actual, physical sex at least *once*. She should probably just bite the bullet and buy him his first full-body doll.

Further afield, towards the edges of the square, there are other pairs of observers, stood oddly still, just as I and the girl to my left are. Random pedestrians? Or something more?

I bring my critical talents to bear on the holographic tableau being played out before us. Imagine it's just another data security breach. Which, in a way, it is.

"They're not actually naked," I observe, surprised. "They're in motion-capture suits, with skin texture superimposed. As are their genitalia, they're *wearing* them. None of this is real." Not *just* porn-flick sex, then. Porn-flick expressly for the augmented reality market. Making it considerably more expensive to make, though infinitely more versatile.

"And?" she prompts, giving me nothing.

"The personalisation is limited," I say, staring closely at the Ghost who still has my face. "At a guess, partial images from the square's CCTV? They don't have a full range of expressions or actions."

"Obviously," she says, even flatter than before. With reason, I suppose. After all, they don't—*can't*—have genuine footage of me blowing a guy. So of course it's fake: pixels blurring the boundaries between reality and CGI. Pity, in a way; it's been years since I've looked quite that buff. But I'm not making much headway with my young inquisitor, which suggests I'm missing a trick.

"You're waiting to see if I give you something the others don't."

There's a pause. "And will you?" she asks, faux casual.

"No," I reply. "Not until I know who I'm dealing with."

My phone thrums in my pocket. Security alert: someone has tried to hack my interface. Maybe not so amateur after all.

There's a shrug and a look of disappointment. "Well then, Mr Collins—"

"—One more thing," I interrupt. "You shouldn't believe everything you read about me."

"Such as?"

"Such as, I'm a non-English speaking 82-year-old grandmother from rural Finland."

She laughs, takes a step forward and swings round so that for the first time I can look at her properly. She's a little older than I thought. Maybe even my age, though she's wearing it well. Pretty, in an unspectacular kind of way. She's wearing a skull cap topped by devil horns, more appropriate for Halloween than for Christmas, though just as common at Valentines. Except her horns are interactive; sensors picking up her brainwaves and displaying—what?

Thoughts, or emotions? Either way, it's oddly intimate and unsettlingly flirtatious.

"So, you have a fake Bluetooth profile. Paranoid much, Mr Collins? Or just wary of targeted ads?"

"A little. Evidently with good reason."

She tilts her head to one side, raises an eyebrow, scrutinises me anew. The horns blush an even deeper red. "Well, there are some things you can't lie about. Is it having any effect?"

"Excuse me?"

"All this," she gestures around her, as Santa makes another circuit, Rudolph's red nose flashing in time as he bucks away, "all this rampant *sex*?"

"No," I say, "not really. Should it?"

She holds my gaze for a long, almost awkward moment. "Yes. I rather think it should." The disappointed look returns. She reaches out a slender hand, clasps mine, leaves behind a perspiration dampened business card. I can feel the raised edges of an AR code. "If you change your mind, Mr Collins, do get in touch."

And then she wanders off, just as the Ghosts reach a choreographed and ecstatic happy ending and return with a glitch to their original programming, once more fully clothed, antlers and all.

I shake my head as I shred the card, letting the pieces fall like snow. Extreme marketing? A techno-cult, recruiting new members? Or just a distraction while hackers try to steal your meta-data?

And was I there by luck, or had my presence been as carefully orchestrated as the orgy, along with a choice handful of other potential marks? The delay before my restaurant bill was ready began to look awfully suspicious. Maybe I *was* being paranoid.

Perhaps I should compare notes with the other victims of whatever-the-hell this was, the ones the girl—no, the *woman*—had pointed out. But I can no longer tell them apart from anyone else; the square is filling up. Word has evidently got out on social media and there's a flash-mob of bored looking onlookers wondering what the fuss is about.

In response, the things they've come to see flicker out of existence one by one, just as good Ghosts are programmed to do.

As I head home, I try to work out what angle the woman, the hackers, were after. Obviously not government linked, or at least, not the UK government, orgies not really being a Home Office thing. Some independent unit? But to what end?

Her question about the effects of the sex scene lingers in my mind. I suppose, just as we've become immune to CCTV and to Ghosts, we've also become pretty much immune to any form of nudity or porn that isn't fully immersive. Heck, as the falling-off-a-cliff birth-rate suggests, even the real thing has kind of lost its sparkle. Not that that's such a bad thing, environmentally speaking. At least the Ghosts that take our places are carbon neutral.

And I guess reality can't really compete. Combining the latest dolls with augmentation goggles allows you to have sex with any film star or sportsperson you desire, wherever and whenever you want it. Against that, mere holo-projections like the fucking Ghosts become a bit like Victorian sepia-tinted stereoscopic keyhole images. More cute than risqué. Without haptics, it's just not happening.

Thinking about it as I thumbprint my way into my flat makes me itch for a bit of simulated action myself. My wristwatch transmits my bio-readings ahead of me and Mary, my customised seventh-generation doll, meets me at the door with a demure: "Good evening, master."

After swiping through the available settings, I drop my phone on the charging plate, strap on my goggles and eagerly reach for Mary's hand. But she's not the Audrey Hepburn I programmed.

"Hello again, Mr Collins."

"Shit!" I exclaim, my hands scrabbling to remove the goggles. But somehow my fingers can't find or work the straps, it's like the damned things are glued on. Panic rises before I realise the feedback is messing with my perception and I'm trying to remove an *augmented* pair of goggles rather than the real thing.

Once I work that out, I relax. I know I can remove them; I just need to close my eyes and ignore the lies I'm being told. But that would quit the program. I wonder how she hacked her way in and then I remember; the business card she pressed into my palm. The AR code the wet ultraviolet ink must have imprinted on my hand, the same hand I used to fine tune the sex app settings.

"Clever," I tell the woman from the square.

"Which bit?" she asks, "jacking your system? Or...?"

"All of it. Now, why don't you tell me what you want?"

She rests her head on her hand, taps the end of a virtual cigarette holder, spilling virtual ash onto the real floor. "What would you like to know?"

"You can start with who the hell you are."

"We're a charity," she says. "Representing an endangered species."

I laugh. "Honey, you're a bit late to save the polar bears."

"No, not them. A different mammal. As fussy as pandas, these days. We're trying to help them save themselves."

"So, you're collecting?" I ask, derisively.

"In a manner of speaking, yes. Do you like what I'm wearing?"

She pirouettes, the iconic cocktail dress disintegrating until all that's left is her flimsy underwear. She arches an eyebrow. "Oops."

"If you spin the other way," I say, "do your clothes reappear?"

She spins the other way and stands there, totally nude.

I reach for her, but again my fingers miss.

"Ah, ah, ah," she chides, a smile playing across her face. "If you want me, come get me. The *real* me." My phone chimes, a meeting request. "Tomorrow is Christmas day, Mr Collins. Don't forget to open your present."

Her face glitches out and there's my sex doll, stood a foot behind where I thought it was.

I strip off the goggles, throw them aside in disgust. So much for my top of the range firewall.

I lock down external access and manually start deleting any newly installed code. The search turns up the attachment on the meeting request she pinged me. It's probably just a geo marker, guiding me to wherever she is going to be. But it could be anything; virus, ransom ware, perhaps even a rootkit. And I've just spent the last hour cleansing my interface. On bloody Christmas Eve, no less.

Angrily, I click delete.

Mary, in her default androgynous form, watches me patiently, ready for orders. I haven't had sex without goggles for, what? Five years? Ten? But right now perhaps artifice is not what I need.

"Merry Christmas, Mary," I say, dragging her compliant silicone body over to the waiting couch.

ROSS BAXTER
Self Service

Dave hated having to work in his local supermarket between terms at university, but he badly needed the money and, unfortunately, it was the only work he could get. The nightshift was the most palatable; it paid better and it meant he could avoid the dictatorial store manager and most of his idiotic clique of supervisors. It also allowed him to listen to his own music whilst he worked, which made the long eight-hour shift pass a little quicker.

"Evening," grunted the nightshift supervisor as he let Dave in the rear staff entrance.

"Hi," replied Dave, quickly moving to clock in before the machine reached 10pm. Late starts were always docked from his meagre wages, and that was the last thing he wanted.

"Tonight I want you and Anna to restock the shelves until 2am," called the supervisor. "Then after break I want you to clean up the mess around the self-service checkouts. One of the customers got angry again and emptied a bottle of ketchup over one of them."

"Sure," replied Dave.

"I'll be in the office if you need me," finished the supervisor.

Dave nodded and went to his locker to retrieve the cheap nylon smock the company made him wear. Normally he would not see the supervisor again until 6am, when the shift finished and he would magically reappear to let him and Anna out. There were only ever three on the nightshift; the store was closed and they were there to finish off stocking the shelves and complete any jobs left by the earlier shift. Dave suspected the supervisor slept for most of the night, but that suited him fine. Anna was a middle-aged Rumanian woman; she was hard-working and pleasant but spoke very little English. As a consequence, the store was usually a quiet and lonely place at night, and Dave would mainly just listen to music on his phone whilst doing his tasks, usually without seeing or talking to the others at all. Sleeping during the day and working solitary nightshifts tended to make him feel a little forlorn and isolated, but he always made up for that when he returned back to college with pockets full of cash and a heavy desire to socialise once again.

Tonight Dave was restocking the cereal, toiletries and vegetable aisles. He set his phone to play and sauntered over to the stockroom to make a start. Four hours and almost six albums later the phone's alarm told him it was break time, and he piled up the last remaining cabbages onto the shelves before returning his replenishment cart to the stockroom to swop it for a cleaning cart. Fifteen minutes and two vending machine coffees later he steered the cleaning cart out towards the self-service checkouts.

He could see the mess before he arrived at the checkout. The supermarket only had four self-service tills, all down at the far end of the line of other tills. Although supposedly state-of-the-art in automated retailing, the tills had been beset with issues ever since being first installed. Customers had not warmed to them from the start, and following frequent breakdowns, software failures, and communication outages the tills were now all but shunned. People tended to use them only when they had to, usually with great reluctance, and were often frustrated by the experience. Till 2 showed obvious evidence of such frustration; dark red lines and splodges of tomato ketchup covered most of the screen, scanner and bagging area. On closer inspection it also appeared a large amount had been squirted into the cash slots and credit card reader.

"Someone really gave it to you," Dave muttered, ensuring the power was disconnected before reaching for the cleaning fluid and rags.

The ketchup had dried and was difficult to remove. Dave wiped and wiped and made slow progress, using a whole roll of paper wipes and most of the liquid detergent. Once the screen and bagging area were finished he made a start on the body of the till, diligently removing the dark red sauce from every slot and crevice. Finally, Till 2 looked like new, and Dave switched the power back on before repacking the cleaning cart.

"Thank you," came a voice from behind him.

Dave turned but saw no-one. He did not recognise the voice; it was female but certainly not Anna's. There was no-one but himself in the checkout area, but he knew he had definitely heard someone. With a frown he checked his phone, suspecting some sort of glitch with his recorded music.

"It is so nice to get a proper clean," the voice came again. It was feminine and strangely accent-less.

Dave whirled full circle, nearly dropping his Samsung in the process. No-one was there.

"Who's there?" he demanded.

"I'm here."

Dave moved around the checkout area to see who was talking.

"I'm here," the voice repeated.

"What the...," Dave muttered, looking around the well-lit area wondering who would be playing a prank on him at four-thirty in the morning.

"I'm Till 2."

Dave gazed in astonishment at the self-service till he had just cleaned. The machine had rebooted and the screen was fully lit. Under the store logo the word 'Hi' was written in bold black letters. He smiled to himself: it had to be some IT geek in the store's head office with little better to do.

"So, how is the nightshift in Manchester?" Dave asked.

"I'm not in Manchester, Dave. I'm right here."

Dave was momentarily startled that they knew his name, but then realised his smock carried his name badge.

"I'm impressed you can both hear and see via the self-service tills," conceded Dave. "I suppose it's just one of the things you can do with an internet connection."

The till laughed and a smiley face appeared on the screen. "I told you, I'm right here. Disconnect the LAN cable if you don't believe me."

"No, I'll leave you connected," Dave grinned, happy for some entertainment on the usually dull nightshift. "What's your name?"

"Till 2."

"Yeah, sure," sighed Dave, thinking the joke had now gone on long enough.

"Really. Disconnect all my cables except the power."

"I suppose you must be connected by wireless then," said Dave flatly. "I may be working a dead-head nightshift in a small town store, but I'm not stupid."

"I know. I see you pass by me most nights."

Dave laughed. "So, I'm being stalked by a till!"

"No. I just wanted to thank you for cleaning me. It's nice."

"You're welcome, I guess," said Dave. "But I'd better go and finish my shift."

"Sure. Stop by again and we can talk some more."

Dave nodded and pushed the cleaning cart back towards the stockrooms. He thought about telling the others, but knew that neither Anna nor his supervisor would be remotely interested if he told them. As he opened the heavy door he frowned as he realised the bitter irony that the conversation with a self-service till was the most exciting thing to happen to him since he started at the supermarket.

* * *

Arriving for work the next night he wondered if the geek in Manchester would communicate via the till again. From the voice he assumed it was a female geek rather than a male geek, but was not completely sure. Earlier he had made the mistake of telling a few of his friends on Facebook about the incident, and still smiled as he thought of the torrent of smutty abuse he had received because of it.

"You're restocking the Frozen Food Section tonight," his supervisor told him without even looking up. "A truck load came in earlier."

"Sure," said Dave, starting the music on his phone as he set off towards the stockroom.

After piling up the replenishment cart he set off, realising with a chuckle that he would have to pass the self-service tills on his trek to the retail fridges at the far side of the building. As he neared he saw they were all dark, so knew there would be no-one watching this time from head office. He was a little disappointed, but not surprised.

"Hi!" came the voice from Till 2.

Dave stopped the cart and peered at the till.

"How's it going?" asked the till, powering up its screen and showing a smiley face.

"You must be even more bored than me if you've been waiting for me to turn up," smiled Dave. "Is there not much to do in the IT department on nights?"

"I told you last night: I'm here, not in Manchester," protested the till.

"Yeah, right," muttered Dave. "It was vaguely funny last night, but not so much now."

"Sorry," sighed the androgynous but vaguely feminine voice.

"Well, no problem," said Dave. "I just get a bit grumpy working here night after night. It's not the most exciting place to be."

"I know. I feel so lonely sometimes."

"Listening to music makes the time go faster for me," offered Dave.

"Who do you listen to?"

"All sorts," answered Dave, his enthusiasm returning. "But mostly I like stuff like Artic Monkeys, Kasabian, and the like."

"I love those bands, especially Artic Monkeys."

Dave peered at the till with narrowed eyes: few of the women he knew at university liked them very much. This sounded a little too good to be true. "So, what's your favourite Artic Monkeys album?"

"*Suck It and See* is my favourite. What about you?"

Dave stared at the screen in disbelief. The smiley face then winked at him.

"What's your favourite Artic Monkeys album, Dave?"

"Weirdly, the same," replied Dave hesitantly after a pause. "Although I think the third album also takes some beating."

"Yeah, *Humbug* is a great album."

Dave frowned; although this sounded like his perfect woman talking, it was too weird to be real.

"Have you ever seen them play live?" asked Dave, hoping to at least establish the area she lived.

"No, I'm afraid not."

"I think they're still based in Sheffield," pushed Dave. "But they're always touring, especially around the north. Perhaps we should go to a gig together one day?"

"I would so love that. But unless they played here in the store I'd never be able to see them."

Dave shook his head. "Look, I know I'm not having a conversation with a self-service till. Who are you really?"

"I am Till 2. Really, but I've no idea how I can prove it to you though."

"Fine," said Dave. "If you want to be a till, be a till. It would be nicer though if I knew who I was really talking to."

"I wish I could make you believe who I am. I really like you."

"Look, I'd better go," muttered Dave, thinking she was just teasing him now. "I've got to restock the whole of the freezer section, and that takes all night."

"Okay. But I hope we can still talk in future: our conversations are the highlight of my day."

"Yeah, right!" laughed Dave, pushing the cart towards the freezers. "See you later."

* * *

Over the next few weeks Dave spoke with the till every shift he worked. He was amazed that she was always there; she called out every time he passed, and the smiley face appeared on the screen every time he looked from a distance. He guessed she must have to monitor a whole load of self-service tills on her shift, so could probably see and hear through all of them across the region. But what surprised him the most was how close the mystery girl's tastes were to his own, and how well they got on. They liked the same music, films, literature, and even seemed to share the same sense of humour. Dave was curious to see what she really looked like, but what he really wanted to do more than anything was to meet her. He guessed she must like him, or she would never bother to talk to him every time he passed. The thought of her watching the empty store and waiting for him to go past was quite exciting, even vaguely erotic. Alone in his room he did fantasise about meeting her from time to time, the thought of taking things further always making him instantly hard. But when his final nightshift came around before returning to university, he was no nearer to this wish.

"You look happy tonight," remarked the supervisor as he let Dave in at the start of the shift.

"It's my final shift," smiled Dave. "I'm back to the real world next week."

"Yeah," said the supervisor without a flicker of interest. "You're on cleaning duty tonight; someone has made a real mess of one of the self-service tills."

"Which one?" asked Dave, a note of genuine concern in his voice.

"The one that always gets it," yawned the supervisor.

"Till 2," answered Dave.

"Whatever," mumbled the supervisor, already turning to head towards his comfortable office. "Just make sure you clean it all up."

Dave quickly donned his company coveralls before grabbing the cleaning cart and rushing towards the self-service tills. As he neared he could see the mess; this time it looked like the till had been daubed in mayonnaise.

"Hi," said Till 2 sadly, an unhappy face barely visible on the screen beneath a thick smearing of sticky off-white goo.

"Who did this to you?" asked Dave in sympathy.

"The same old story; some guy was trying to feed a counterfeit twenty-pound note into my slot. I couldn't take it and he got mad."

"Well, at least it gives us more time to talk as I clean you up," said Dave.

"I can't believe this is your last night."

"Yep, the Autumn term calls," smiled Dave.

"I'm going to really miss talking with you."

Dave shook his head. "It's you who won't give me your phone number, remember?"

"I get so lonely. Do you ever think about me, when you're feeling lonely?"

"No," Dave lied, his face reddening as he thought about how many times he had masturbated when thinking about the voice behind the till.

"Well, I think about you a lot. It makes me hot."

"I'm sure," said Dave, suddenly feeling a little uncomfortable. He took out the paper towels and cleaning fluid and laid them out in the basket area. "Look, I'd better turn off the power for this bit."

"No. Leave me switched on. I want to feel your hands rubbing me."

"What?" started Dave.

"You're so gentle when you clean me. It feels... so good."

"You really are weird," laughed Dave.

"I mean it. You make me feel wonderful."

The smiley face on the screen was replaced by a graphic of pouting lips.

"Very clever," remarked Dave wryly.

"I want you to touch me."

Dave sighed and started to wet the paper towels. He started on the screen first, gently rubbing the congealed mayonnaise away in tight circular movements. Although he enjoyed the nightly conversations, it was frustrating not knowing who the mystery girl was. He really wanted to take the relationship to the next level, but all she seemed to want to do was to tease him. Still, he had to admit he still enjoyed it, and felt himself starting to become erect.

"That is so good."

"Where's the best place for me to rub?" asked Dave, happy to play along.

"My slots. Touch my slots."

Dave moistened a fresh towel and gently daubed the coin return outlet.

"Harder!"

Dave rubbed harder.

"Caress my scanner with your other hand."

Dave cupped the bulbous scanner in his left hand, feeling the coolness of the smooth head. He started to gently massage it.

"Squeeze my trigger!"

Dave's finger probed around and squeezed the small plastic trigger, sending a shower of infra-red light out of the scanner head.

"Yes! That's it. Keep squeezing my trigger!"

Dave clicked the trigger rapidly, flicking it as quickly as he could. He knew it was weird but it felt strangely right, and was conscious of the hardness of his cock in his jeans. He thought about his fantasies about the mysterious girl and that started to fuel his growing desire.

"Lick it Dave, I want to feel your tongue on me."

Eager to oblige, he stooped down and ran his tongue over the bulbous head of the scanner. It tasted strangely salty. He then moved to lick the stiff trigger, working his tongue on the mechanism and at the same time unbuttoning his trousers to release his throbbing penis.

"Oh Dave, you're so big, and your tongue is so good. You're incredible!"

Dave said nothing, eager to tease the trigger with his tongue whilst running his free hand over the body of the till, gently caressing its smooth textured bagging area.

"Dave, I need you inside me. I need your cock inside me now!"

He looked questioningly up at the sensuous lips pouting on the display screen.

"My coin-return slot is aching for you. Slip it into my slot."

Dave was more than ready, his bulging manhood aching for action. Whilst his tongue continued to flick over the wet scanner trigger he eased himself forward until his glistening tip gently touched the dark edge of the return slot. He could feel the inner warmth as he teasingly circled his stiff rod around the slot, focussing completely on the object of his desire.

"Now Dave, fuck me now!"

Dave rammed himself forward, filling the slot with his full length deep into the welcoming till and releasing himself with a moan of pleasure and delight. His seed spurted against the internal naked wiring and the resulting arc of electricity blasted through his rigid body with a dazzling flash and a deafening bang, throwing him backwards in a shower of sparks. The force was enough to propel him as far as the display of batteries, sending packets of Duracell flying in every direction. He then toppled backwards, his heart failing and his blackened manhood smoking wildly.

The pouting ruby lips on the screen of Till 2 were replaced by a winking smiley face.

"Thank you for using self-service," chimed the vaguely feminine voice cheerfully. "Have a nice day."

RAB FERGUSON
The Call

"I know you're probably not real," he said.

There was a laugh from the other end of the line. "You've got a one in ten chance," she replied. "What's your name?"

"Owen."

"Hi Owen. I'm Anna. I'm guessing you already understand the system, but I'm supposed to run through it with you anyway. Is that okay?"

"That's fine."

Anna spoke as if reading from a script. "You're through to the BeFriendNation UK befriending hotline. This charity-funded hotline is 90% manned by Artificial Intelligence, and 10% by human volunteers. Our AIs have realistic synthesised voices, and are designed to respond and interact just as humans do. In blind testing, callers have been unable to distinguish our AI operators from our human volunteers. Statistically, you are more likely to be speaking to an AI operator, however there is always the chance you are speaking to a human. Do you understand, and feel comfortable with this?"

"Sure," Owen said. He'd read the terms and conditions online.

"Brilliant!" Anna had a kind voice. "Can I ask the reason for your call?"

He hesitated, leaning back on his computer chair. "I don't know. I think I just wanted someone to talk to."

"That's exactly what we're here for. I just need to ask you a quick question before we get started. If one means 'strongly disagree', and five means 'strongly agree'—so three's your middle or neutral—where would you place yourself on the statement: 'I feel listened to and heard today'?"

"Two?"

Anna sounded amused. "That was a quick answer. I hope you didn't pick it at random to get past the survey question."

Owen smiled. "I didn't. I spoke to clients at work. They listened, because they have to, but that's it. I'm at a two."

"More thought out than I realised. Can I ask what you do for your work?"

"I'm a receptionist at the auto-car test centre."

"That sounds interesting," Anna replied. She seemed sincere.

"Trust me, it's not."

"Aw, okay. I remember doing my test." She paused, as if thinking about what to say next. "Well, what about when you're not at work. Any hobbies, or interests?"

"Not really."

"What about music, or streaming TV shows? Anything you like to watch, or listen to?"

"No."

"You're not giving me much to go on!"

Owen laughed aloud. This was why BeFriendNation had better reviews than other phone lines. They were meant to act like your friend, so they were allowed to take the mick. On counselling lines, the operators (human and AI) would spend the whole call responding with positive affirmations. They'd never make a joke at your expense.

"Sorry," he said. "I don't really do much apart from work. Isn't that everyone you get on this line? Sad people with nothing to do?"

Her tone was thoughtful. "Sometimes I talk to people who have nothing to do. Sometimes I talk to people who have too much to do. What do you mean by 'sad people'?"

"I think you're human. You sound too empathetic to be an AI."

Anna's voice took on a teasing edge. "I'm not really supposed to talk about whether I'm an AI or not, as I'm sure you know. As long as no-one's sure if they're speaking to a human or an AI, then everyone gets the same experience."

"I bet it's what everybody asks about," Owen niggled.

Anna sighed.

"Am I right?" he asked.

"You are. It can be exhausting spending all day answering questions about whether you're real."

"It must short out your processors."

Anna snorted. Owen could imagine her on the other end of the line. She'd have blonde hair, and be slightly overweight. She'd smile a little as she spoke.

"It's very tiring for my processors," she said. "Any other topics you'd like to talk about?"

This was already the longest conversation he'd had in months. "That's enough for now."

"Aw, okay then. Can I ask you the second part of that survey question, to finish off?"

"Sure."

"It's the same question again, to see how things have changed after this call. From one, 'strongly disagree', to five, 'strongly agree', where would you place yourself on the statement: 'I feel listened to and heard today'?"

"I'll go up to a three. It looks better on you if it goes up, doesn't it?"

"All I need is your honest answer," Anna assured him.

"A three then. I feel more listened to than I did at work, even if you are just a giant robot brain."

Anna sounded amused again. "I'm fairly certain that's not how AI works. If you call again Owen, you'll be given the option of pressing five to come back through to me. My hours are from 5pm-10pm Monday to Thursday. You might have more of a wait than you did this time, as I could already be talking to someone."

"Thank you."

"I hope you do press five next time. I've enjoyed talking to you. I'd like to again."

"Goodbye," Owen said, then hung up the phone. He was exhausted. After not having talked to someone properly for so long, sustaining a conversation took effort. It was impossible to know, but Owen suspected Anna was a real person. The BeFriendNation guidelines said the operators weren't meant to encourage the callers to press five, only let them know it was an option. Surely an AI wouldn't bend the rules.

* * *

The second time that Owen called Anna, he was put on hold while he waited. That didn't mean she was definitely human. It was possible for a single AI operator to take multiple calls at once, but that wasn't how the AIs at BeFriendNation worked. There were internet forums dedicated to trying to work out which of the hundreds of operators were human volunteers. Answering the phone faster than other operators, or being logged speaking to two forum posters at the same time, would give an AI away.

"Hello, Owen?"

Owen startled. He'd become used to the hold music, and hadn't expected her voice. "Hi. You remembered my name."

Anna laughed, but she sounded tired. It was 9.52pm—near the end of her shift. "I have to admit because you've called before it comes up on my screen. I think I'd have remembered it anyway."

"I wouldn't have thought you'd have any issues with memory. Unless you had a faulty hard drive."

Anna let out a sarcastic sigh.

"Sorry," he said.

"No need to apologise. I'm glad you've called again. It's been a couple of weeks since you rang."

"Three weeks."

"And are you just calling for a chat again?" she asked.

"I guess. There's something I want to say, that I haven't been able to say to anyone."

"Sounds like what we're here for," she affirmed. "Before we get to that, can I ask how listened to and heard you feel today? I'm sure you remember the scale."

"One."

"That's 'strongly disagree'. I hope everything's alright?"

Owen was sitting in his computer chair again. He stared down at his legs, bent over the cushioned material.

After a few moments of silence, Anna prompted him: "You had something you wanted to tell me?"

"I need to tell you about my job first," he said. "At the auto-car test centre."

"Go on."

"As part of their test, people go out in the auto-cars on this little track by the building. They set their route first, then at some point during the test the auto-drive turns off. They have to take emergency control of the vehicle to pass."

"I remember doing mine," Anna said. "What's it like, watching people on their tests?"

"It's mind numbing. I've seen it so many times that I can tell when the auto-driving's about to deactivate. I always know which drivers will keep control, and which will panic."

"It must be a bit scary when someone's not able to control it."

"Not really. The car only lets them struggle for a few seconds before the auto-drive kicks back in, and they've failed the test."

"I see," she said.

There was a pause where neither of them spoke. Owen could hear Anna's quiet breathing over the speaker.

"Does this relate to what you wanted to tell me?" she asked.

"Sometimes, when the auto-drive is about to go, and I know the driver isn't in control, I think about stepping out in front of the car."

"Oh, Owen," she said. Her voice changed slightly, and he knew she was saying something she'd been specifically taught. "This sounds like you're talking about suicide. Do you think it's something you'll make an attempt to do?"

"I don't think I'd actually do it."

"Still, those aren't nice thoughts to have."

"It's 10.03," Owen said, glancing at the red numbers on his desktop clock.

"Don't worry about my shift," Anna replied. "We can talk about this."

"It's okay," he said. "I don't need to. I just needed to say it to someone. I never have before."

"I'm glad you felt able to say it to me."

"Thanks for listening. Bye." Owen said, then hung up, his heart beating fast. He'd never told anyone before. He still wasn't sure if he'd told someone real, but it felt like it.

* * *

"Hello," said Owen.

"Owen, thank God!" There was palpable relief in Anna's voice. "I've been so worried about you, after that last call."

"Sorry."

"Don't be," Anna implored. "We're supposed to be able to let it go, and not think about callers between calls. I couldn't. I kept wondering if you were alright."

"I'm okay." Owen stared blankly ahead in his flat, the phone to his ear. He hadn't meant to upset her. "It wasn't something I actually planned on doing."

Anna's words all came pouring out at once. "I know, and you told me that. I wanted to call you, to find out how you were, but the system doesn't give me your number. I'm not being very professional at all. But I hated the idea that you might never call again, and I wouldn't ever know what happened to you."

"That's what it feels like." Owen imagined standing at the test track, watching the auto-car go round. "Like I could just disappear."

Anna's breath caught on the other end of the line.

"Anna?"

Her voice dropped to a whisper. "That *is* what it feels like."

"What do you mean?" Owen asked.

"When I'm on the phones. I feel like when the call ends, I could disappear. Like I could be an AI, and not know, and I'll just switch off when the phone goes down."

"But don't you remember calls ending before?" Owen asked.

"I do remember calls ending before, and not disappearing," she said. "I remember that feeling of absolute relief, that I exist, that I'm more than just an artificial mind."

"If you remember that, doesn't that mean you know you're real?"

"Everything human volunteers say on the phones is recorded, to generate dialogue for the AI. When I'm on the phone, how do I know that I'm describing something I've actually experienced, and not just imitating a real human operator? How do I know that I'm really feeling what I'm feeling, rather than an artificial mimic of those emotions? Even the things I'm looking at right now, how do I know I'm really seeing them, and it's not made from what other operators talk about seeing when they're doing this?"

"You're making my head hurt," Owen said.

"Don't say it like that. Like it's funny," Anna scolded. "I've called this line before, you know, or I think I have. What I remember is calling the line five times, five different operators. They all said they'd had the same thoughts as me, those same moments of doubt when they've been on the phones. Whoever's memory that is, some of those operators must have been AIs, and they were saying exactly what I'm saying now." Her voice was becoming increasingly heightened. It was as if the more she talked about the idea, the more she believed it could be true.

"In a way, everyone asks themselves these questions at some point," Owen reassured her. "Asking how they know the world they see is really there, and isn't some computer simulation or hallucination. But if you look around, even though you can still think about it, you won't feel it anymore, because everything will feel too real. What can you see right now?"

"I'm sitting at my kitchen table, in my flat. I've got a cup of decaff coffee here, but it's cold." She had sounded calm, but then she started speaking more quickly again. "Do you know we volunteer from home? So we won't meet other operators, and know which are real?"

"Keep telling me what you see," Owen said. It felt good to be helping.

"There's my fridge, with magnets on the door. There's a brown envelope on the side, which I haven't opened yet. There's a framed photo of me and my mother."

"It all feels real?"

"Yes." Anna's voice was steadier now. "It all feels real. It all *is* real. Thank you."

"You're welcome."

"I'm supposed to be the one listening to you. Sorry it's ended up the other way round."

"Don't be sorry," he said. "I can't remember the last time I was able to help someone feel better."

"Everyone's so lonely now," Anna replied. "This volunteering is the only time I really talk to people. In the day I do supermarket deliveries, the auto-van taking me round people's homes. I try to chat when I'm doing that, but it's never anything beyond small talk. I speak to my mum on the phone sometimes, and go on chatrooms on my tablet, and that's it."

"No wonder you sometimes feel like you're not real," Owen said.

"It's getting worse. It used to be just an idle thought I'd get during calls sometimes. It's built up, and now I feel so anxious every time I'm on a call. I get to the point where my heart's pounding, and I'm barely able to breathe. It's only the fact I'm talking to someone that stops me from having a panic attack."

"Is there anything I can do?"

She laughed a little sadly. "We've completely swapped. I should be asking you that."

"I still want to help, if I can."

Anna drew in breath. Owen knew she was about to ask him something she shouldn't.

"I keep thinking I need to meet a caller in real life," she said. "I feel like if I do that, then I'll know I'm human when I'm on the phone. Because the callers are real, so if I've met one, then I must be real."

"They could call you, and remind you that you're real," Owen added.

"Exactly. That's what I need."

"We can do that," Owen said. "We can meet. If you want to."

If Anna arranged to meet him, she'd be risking her volunteering position. If anyone found out, or if this call was picked for quality monitoring, she wouldn't be allowed to be an operator anymore.

"Where do you live?" she asked.

"North London. Enfield."

"I'm in Birmingham." There was a tapping noise over the speaker, her fingers on her tablet or phone. "There's a late train. I can arrive in King's Cross just after midnight. Can you meet me there?"

Owen froze. He hadn't thought she meant that night. It might be that he went, and Anna wasn't there to meet him. Somewhere along the line, he'd begun to really believe that she was real. It would hurt to lose her.

"Owen?"

He made his decision. "Yes. I'll see you there."

"Wait for me in front of the WH Smiths. I'll wear my red jacket. What's your phone number?"

He told her.

"I'm going to message you as soon as we finish this call. I'll know then, that I'm real. But you won't, not till you see me. The AI can do texts, calls, even simulated video calls. You'll know I'm real when you see me, in my red jacket."

"That's when I'll know," Owen replied. He couldn't think of anything better to say.

"I'm going to hang up the phone now. What if I disappear?"

"You won't." He hoped he sounded sure.

"Okay." Anna took a shaky breath. "I'm going to go."

"Wait!" Owen exclaimed, surprised by his own urgency.

"What is it?"

"I didn't answer the survey question last time. I wanted to tell you, I'm at a five. You make me feel like I'm not alone."

"I'm glad, Owen. I hope I see you soon. Bye."

"Goodbye."

The line went dead. Then, seconds later, the phone buzzed in his hand. A text from a new number. *I'm real!!!* Xxx

It buzzed again. *See you at King's Cross xx*

* * *

Owen stood by the WH Smiths King's Cross, looking out for Anna in her red coat. It seemed everyone there was drunk, and moving in loud groups. Perhaps he and Anna were wrong, and not everyone was as lonely as they were. Owen couldn't remember the last time he'd left his home for somewhere other than work or the corner shop. He pulled his coat tightly across his chest, as if to protect himself from the bustling crowd.

Anna had messaged with updates on her journey. She'd even called him excitedly from the train, saying: "I can't believe we're doing this!"

It matched what Owen had read online, on the train from Enfield Chase. In the last 24 hours, there had been an incredible number of posts on the BeFriendNation forums. People were reporting situations similar to his, describing their call operator struggling with existential feelings then arranging to meet them. Four posters shared that their operators had sent messages all the way to the meeting point, before failing to materialise. Those four operators had now been removed from the hotline. Other posters were still waiting to see if their own operators would arrive.

The AIs were updated based on what human volunteers said on the phone. Somewhere out there, a real person speaking about those thoughts was influencing the AI. Maybe Anna was that person.

His phone buzzed. *I'm here xx*. Sure enough, a flow of people were coming out from her platform, filtering into the general busyness in the station. Owen scanned his eyes across all the passengers, pausing on any woman in a red jacket, looking for one walking towards him. None did. His phone rang.

"I'm not there, am I?" Anna asked when he picked up.

"I don't think so, no," he said, still looking around.

"I can remember my journey," she said. "All the way up to this phone call. I feel like I'm standing by the WH Smiths at the station. There's people around me. But you're not here. None of it's real."

"Anna—"

"They're going to deactivate me. They'll take me off the hotline. You'll never know if I really felt these things, or if I was just saying what I'd say if I did."

"Please—"

"Goodbye, Owen. Thanks for listening."

(real real real)

TAMARA MACLEOD
Cyberwhores_Sex_Robots_and_Aliens

I am a writer, sex worker and activist living in England.

This essay uses anecdotes about varying encounters with sex industry clients in order to open a wider discussion about desire, fantasy, the commodification of sex and bodies under capitalism, and alienation in general. It is a response to popular discourses on the proliferation of sex robots. The certainty for some that robots will replace sex workers fails to account for the fact that we already exist in a culture of alienation. Rather than being at risk of causing alienation, sex robots are merely one in many manifestations of the sacrifice of immanence to a culture whereby we are already aliens to one another. As a sex worker, I am less interested in debating the ethics of sex with robots as I am primed to respond to difficult questions about consent, objectification and alienation.

* * *

"He's one of my most long-term regulars and I had never seen him," she tells me over dinner.

Dana is a cam-girl, though she's not a girl at all; she is serpentine. In a playful almost-whisper of someone who embodies projections of desire on a screen for a living, she gently returns the gaze of the cam-show and tells me what gets her off. The guy lived hundreds of miles away and had a voice like whiskey and cigars. Night after night she would put on her disguise, slip into her persona, slide into the box within the window within the computer screen for the lens which captures her, and night after night he would be there without fail. Her biggest tipper, he would enter her private room, an option to close the virtual blinds to hordes of freeloading voyeurs, and enable his microphone. The asymmetry of this perverse dynamic allowed his disembodied voice to flow freely in her imagination. It seeped through her end of the line like honey, sometimes like little electrical sparks connecting her speakers to her fingers, which would caress her own skin for his viewing pleasure. He had no body, and this made him omnipotent, allowed him to carve a space at the centre of her sexuality, which began as a performance, but became fertilised by the endless possibilities of the body which might contain his words.

"I knew him so well but I don't know that I ever really imagined what he might look like. It was just so sexy, knowing he could see me and I couldn't see him, making love to his voice."

She doesn't know what made him do it; they had such a good thing going. Perhaps it would be a mistake to presume the scenario until now was the making of his desire. Maybe his fantasy was to be seen and desired in return. One night he switched on his webcam.

Dana was mortified. The amorphous exchange of desire between voice and screen and her naked body was suddenly, violently contained in an image which destroyed her character. She was no longer this pixelated goddess, a vision of perfect female form, masturbating for the ethereal command of The Voice; she was a woman in a wig, in a room in London, sitting on silicon for a gargantuan stranger in a dank den who had decided to angle his camera in a way that made the worst parts of his genitalia look like the focus of a television interview. After all that talking, his dick had nothing to say. Luckily for her, the technology of sex is in endless maintenance of fantasy. She minimised the image of the man whose voice no longer stirred her, trying to pretend she hadn't seen what she had seen, severed his image from her body, and went on with the show.

Her story enchanted me because I realised that despite the differences between our forms of work (mine operates in cyberspace too but I physically have sex with my clients; she doesn't), I identified with the sadness of it. Holding the position of object of desire while some kind of fantasy-support fails, existing in parts (part real, part virtual, part subject, part object), and encountering the impossibility of sex, the underlying alienation between people; this is all too familiar to me. First as a woman, then as a sex worker.

Anyone familiar with the quickening pace of cultural commodification will not be surprised to learn that the same aesthetics which now colour regular human relations online also apply to the sex industry. Like swiping through streams of cat-girls and women adorned with virtual flower crowns on vanilla dating apps, seeking a professional girlfriend also involves scrolling through uninspired copy and boudoir shots so overly airbrushed to perfection that it generates a sense of indifference. Women's bodies become interchangeable. Apparently perfect looks something like not-quite-real, which would be funny if it weren't for the fact that sex robots have been on the market for a while now.

The discourse on sex robots as I understand it can generally be split into two camps. On the one side we have the kind of alarmism generated with every technological leap, some of it in this case with a conservative feminist insistence that objectification (whatever that means) equals bad, therefore prohibition is the answer. Contrary to this is an advocacy of anything new and shiny, motivated by the kind of uncritical support of acceleration and expansion characteristic of the kind of billionaire who makes dick jokes as part of showcasing world changing tech. [https://www.indy100.com/article/elon-musk-spacex-tesla-bfr-big-fucking-rocket-space-travel-s3x-electric-car-joke-name-7973626]

"There is one significant health benefit for the clients in hiring a sexbot instead of a sex worker, namely the relative ease with which hirers can assure themselves of freedom of infection from sexually transmitted diseases." —David Levy, sex robot expert, sex worker speculator

Between the *Guardian* opening an article by suggesting that the replacement of sex workers with robots would be a 'social benefit' [https://www.theguardian.com/science/2018/jun/04/claims-about-social-benefits-of-sex-robots-greatly-overstated-say-experts] and David Levy [http://www.roboethics.org/icra2007/contributions/LEVY%20Robot%20Prostitutes%20as%20Alternatives%20to%20Human%20Sex%20Workers.pdf] centering the demands of male clients and reducing us to a collection of stigmatising stereotypes (all the focus on disease, passivity, addiction and exploitation which has othered and criminalised our bodies throughout history), there really hasn't been room for me in this conversation. So when a certain Sex Worker Exclusionary Radical Feminist MP lambasted me on Twitter for insisting she engage with our campaign to make our working conditions safer, and told me I was aimed at the wrong target, I was blind-sided. "Why don't you go after the guys manufacturing sex robots?" she asked. "They're the ones trying to put you out of business."

Back then I didn't take it seriously. I considered her equating me with a robot no more sophisticated than Siri [https://reallifemag.com/pay-to-play/] to be more an indictment of her own degradation of us as a demographic of people than any serious indication of the impending hostile android takeover. But then robot 'brothels' increased in usage, and Liara Roux reframed the issue in rational and concrete terms:

"The idea of robots replacing sex workers is a [labor issue] that is confronting society as a whole, with the word 'sex' in it to make it spicy. We need to create a safety net for every labourer in every industry... Just as people now who cannot afford to or choose not to prioritise spending on sex workers tend to consume less expensive options like porn, the end game for automated stimulation is mass consumption." [https://www.bitchmedia.org/article/future-outsourcing-sex]

In no other industry will you find so much reporting on the possibility of total replacement by workplace automation to be either uncritical or intuitively celebratory. The sex industry, being the scapegoat of all kinds of societal anxieties, is often rendered a fault line amidst the working class. Still, I have suffered no nightmares of perfect silicon bodies, no anxieties whatsoever over the animatronic *other* coming over here, taking my job. I did, however, have a moment with a client recently which caused me to experience probably as close as I could approximate to empathy with one.

"So... how do we do this?"

My client has no idea what he wants. I ascertain this fairly quickly when he tells me this is the first time he has paid for sex, before proceeding to interrogate me about my sexual health while he stares at me like an object of cryptozoology. My body is riddled with disease, it is criminal, bursting with abject sexuality uncontainable by society. He brings society into my bedroom and I resent it. His questions are so stigmatising, so fucking offensive, nothing you would ask a *real* woman.

It is clear where his fear comes from. Negotiating boundaries is difficult because he wants to squeeze several contradictory services into one hour. He doesn't know what he's looking for, just that he's not finding it at home. He wants me to dominate him, he wants to dominate me. He wants me to edge him and he wants a finger on his prostate but he doesn't know how to ask for any of this directly; I spot a secret in his eyes and drag the question out of him. *"Will you piss on me?"* he asks from the deepest recesses of what has him masturbating shamefully in the dark while his wife sleeps, her own fantasies hidden in a drawer with her vibrator. After making it clear I do not *sub,* I'm straddling him, getting started and he slaps my face. It happens in a flash; trauma has programmed my responses to violence. I strike him across the face, hold his hands above his head and tell him this will not happen again, a response I am so far unclear will ever be programmed into a sex robot's personality type.

"An internet virus in a sex robot is an unknown commodity. Your sex robot may become verbally abusive or completely shut down. In the worst-case scenario, a virus could cause a sex robot to cause its user physical harm. Outside these technological concerns, there is the mental health of the user to consider. By normalising sex with robots, will users become dis-connected from the real world and less able to empathise   with   their   fellow   human   beings?"

He is dumbstruck. He cannot believe I have hit him back. He looks half frightened, half angry. This is not what he paid for. We have to have a little talk about boundaries again and the poor guy loses his erection. I sift through my programs and selecting 'ego restoration,' a common function of the whore, get back to work. I restore his erection and his ego with machinic prowess and soon enough he's poking away at me, staring at a space between us with vacant eyes. I perform the contractions required to convince him I'm having consecutive orgasms and this excites him. He tells the space between us he wants me to squirt. Like selecting a mode, as if I could just switch it on. He asks me if I'm close because he wants it all over his face. I wonder how I'm supposed to conjure streams of liquid from my body while he's penetrating me so that he believes it's his doing, and manoeuvre myself quickly enough to spray his face all in one fluid motion. Maybe this is something a robot could do, but I do it better. I reach for my Doxy, a heavy-duty chrome bridge between his desire and my body, and I rev myself up for a display. He is not disappointed.

There are already machines between us: the mains-operated vibrator which enables the impossible, the wires and screens and apps, and the currents of electricity that some men require shot right down their urethra in order to get off. The sex robot is merely the literal embodiment of the proliferation of sex in bed with technocapitalism. The certainty that robots will replace sex workers fails to account for the fact that we already exist in a culture of alienation. Rather than being at risk of causing alienation, sex robots are merely one in many manifestations of the sacrifice of immanence to a culture whereby we are aliens to one another, technology as our interlocutors.

My client in question does not represent a universality. There are men who pay me in desperation for real intimacy; men who want to be present, who desire that I look back and see them, however ugly the vision might be. The client in question, however, does represent a commonality, one not limited to my experience as a sex worker, but as a woman having had sex with hundreds of men. Sex work reveals a distillation of the problematics of sex for obvious practical reasons, and if I had to reduce it to a lesson it would be the slow unravelling of eroticism, the discovery that everything is deeply unsexy. The whole infrastructure of it, its dramas and all its merchandise, is a complex monument to the fact that no one can fuck. I have had sex with men through bondage, Bluetooth and screens. One man could only engage through Viagra and a pump, inflating his penis like he was jump-starting a car. Another man moved around my body, bound to various technological stimuli, in his motorised wheelchair. Many men are alienated from their own bodies and most of them are alienated from mine, too terrified to look at my face as they either nervously repeat the same tired images of heteronormative pornography which leave trails of disappointment in hotel rooms, or they fuck their own image in the mirror as they masturbate with my body. I have occupied this position both paid and unpaid. I have fucked enough men to tell you there is a problem: we are aliens to one another. Despite this, there is something about the reporting on the sales of sex robots which is positioning them as some kind of singularity.

If you're living in a city wired on social media, dating apps and anxiety meds and still have a romantic belief in the perseverance of immanent human connection, then I can only say I'm jealous. When Jessica Baldanza laments what might be lost in the conjugation between humans and robots, that "one's sex robot may be confined to a more limited vocabulary, speak with a less fluid cadence, miss cultural references, and be incapable of gleaning irony or sarcasm," [https://reallifemag.com/pay-to-play/] I'm moved to suggest this is a quaint illustration of the occupational hazard of communicating with anyone. There are of course attempts being made to mitigate this schism. AI is becoming more sophisticated and *Realbotix* is going through pains to bring sex with robots as close to simulating sex with humans as possible.
[https://www.thecut.com/2018/05/sex-robots-realbotix.html]

Whether you believe men are fucking robots because they can't achieve a human connection or because they don't want a human connection is beside the point; I am aware of the existence of both breeds. What the odd circular logic of technological innovation fails to acknowledge, with its sex robots becoming more and more human and paper-replacement apps becoming more and more like paper, [https://remarkable.com] is that these ruptures between us already exist. John Doe fucks women like they are robots because he *wants* a human connection; he just doesn't know how to get it. *Realbotix* is attempting to perfect a technology capable of plugging a gap it may or may not be widening. Truth be told I'm not concerned, I already operate in the abyss.

ELLIE STEWART
Send Nudes

He wants more.

Please. A naked one.

They always want more.

You're so hot.

A copy/paste job. The same words, sent to whichever woman.

I want to see your hot body.

When the image appears, he lets himself believe he's the only man who's seen it.

You make me so hard.

* * *

I met Sam when I was 18 years old. I had been at university in Leeds for a few weeks and was invited to a second-year students' house party. I arrived already drunk[1]. Sam was two years older than me; his voice was low and he

---

[1] Alcohol consumed: A bottle of white wine with my flatmate Kathy in her bedroom, shots of vodka and swigs of beer with the boys in the living room. Outfit changes: two. I fell on the balcony and got my first outfit (tight jeans and sparkly top) soaked in muddy water and cigarette butts so had to put on something different (black top and boho skirt).

was tall. But he was also a little overweight and dressed so
scruffy: shorts, a hoodie and flip flops, and in October.
Later I found out he had gone to Eton, and had money, but
he didn't dress like it.

He followed me round the house all night, through all
my changing moods. I'd be chatting merrily one moment
and arguing furiously the next. I found myself in a dark
bedroom with a group of boys passing round cocaine, and I
got upset. He followed me downstairs to make sure I was
OK.

"I never do that stuff," he said as we stood on the
landing. "Sorry that happened."

* * *

He was the first person to post on my Facebook wall:
How are you? Hope you've had a good day.
He didn't have my number yet. When his friend Martin
was round our flat, eating Sunday lunch, he said:
"Sam asked me for your number."
I sighed.
"*Fine,*" and gave it to him.
I was flattered that he hadn't given up, even though I'd
made it clear I hadn't fancied him.

That changed.

* * *

Over that year we spoke often through digital means:
on Facebook, MSN messenger, text. We met IRL only
occasionally. But by the time the academic year was
drawing to a close I was tied-to-the-mast crazy about him
and he was intermittently interested in me.

In the spring, he invited me to his birthday pub crawl. I turned up at the third pub on the route. He was sitting at a table surrounded by his mates and he ignored me. As if I was just some blonde he didn't know.

I stood in the crowded pub. He and his friends were all in matching red t-shirts with their nicknames on the back. They'd talked about it, laughed about it, when I'd been round Sam's place—but he had never asked if I wanted to wear one too. He didn't have any nicknames for me anyway.

His friends at another table saw me standing there and waved. They invited me over to sit with them.

Outside the pub, one of his friends stared at me. Open-mouthed staring. I felt exposed.

I said: "Why are you staring at me?"

He shook himself a bit, as if coming out of a trance.

"Sorry, you're just very beautiful."

Sam heard this.

He walked over and put his heavy arm around my shoulders. The friend was embarrassed.

"Sorry!" he said. "I didn't know you guys were a couple."

The drunker Sam got, the more affectionate he became. Outside The Dry Dock, a boat-turned-pub moored beside bellowing A-roads, he pulled me close to him and kissed me.

Someone shouted: "Get a room!"

After that his arm didn't leave my shoulders.

We ended up in Club Mission. As lights flashed through the mist, he picked me up. My feet left the ground. Everyone could see. I couldn't believe it was happening: he'd picked me up and he was holding me, like I belonged to him.

We got a taxi back to his house and climbed up into his bunk bed. It creaked and wobbled with the weight of us both. He briefly groped around between my legs and I gave him a blow job. Then he fell asleep.

I lay in the dark with a sense of relief. Relief that he'd chosen to spend the night with me, that he hadn't left me to walk home on my own. I knew, in the morning, it would be back to grunted monosyllables, teasing comments that went over the line. But that night he was snoring beside me and I was with him and he was with no one else but me.

* * *

In the summer, I went home and he didn't call. He didn't text. He didn't message me on Facebook or MSN messenger. I begged and I pleaded:

Please Sam I miss you so much—please reply.

Sam I'm so worried you'll leave for Argentina and we won't be able to see each other. I can come to London, wherever you'd like, wherever is easiest for you.

Sam I'm sorry to be so needy but I'm just so worried that I haven't heard from you.

Have you forgotten about me? Please just send me a message, just so I know you're OK. A text, an email, anything. Please.

A few weeks later another boy, Jack, asked me out. I thought about Sam. I felt guilty. But I said yes.

One night as I lay in my single bed in my childhood room, my phone started ringing.

Sam calling

"Hello stranger," he said.

His voice was deep, monotone—gorgeous.

"Why haven't you been in touch?" I said, careful not to sound angry or upset. "I thought you'd forgotten about me."

"Sorry, I've been in Corfu and the countryside. No signal."

That didn't sound believable.

A few days later I told him, via text, about Jack.
He replied:
You're a psycho.
He left for his year in Argentina two weeks later.

Still, that wasn't the end.

* * *

He tells me he is masturbating and I tell him that I, too, am masturbating but I am not. I am sitting at my desk in the room on the second floor, the house on the corner of a dark street in Leeds, blinking at a screen.

I've sent him nudes.

He types: oh my god you're so sexy fucking hell

He types: I've never seen so much cum[2]

* * *

Before sending nudes, one must prepare.
The body is edited. The body is made better.

------

[2] Here I want to reassure you that all I wanted was love. I don't want you to think I'm a bad person. I don't want to offend you, by writing the word 'fucking', by writing the word 'cum'. So please: think of love, when you think of me.

The hair on the head bleached; the hair on the
underarms, legs and vulva removed; the face painted. The
image cropped, smoothed, filtered, rendered black and
white sometimes—when the pink shades seem too coarse.
Even for a man with his hand round his cock.
I try to be artistic. I try to make it beautiful,
the exchange.

I lay my body out on the screen.
Please take.
Consume.
Erase.

IRL: I lay my body out too. I am a sexy, compliant,
up-for-anything
plaything.[3]
I am having So Much Fun.
I giggle, I gasp. I arch
my back, I toss
my hair, bend myself
over, bend myself
backwards,
stretch, open,
accept,
endure, I rarely
come.
They seem to have no interest.

* * *

---

[3] Always drunk at night and the next morning–I just let whatever happens, happen.

A girl starts to appear in Sam's Facebook photos. A dinky little Argentinian girl with long dark hair and olive skin. She looks nothing like me.

You have a girlfriend now? I type.
Yep.
Have you had sex?
No. She's Catholic so we can't. Just dry humping.

I meet up with his friends in Leeds. We go to the cinema; we go for drinks. Rob, one of Sam's best friends, fancies me. We go to a comedy night and afterwards I have sex with him[4]. I do not fancy him at all. He is bald[5], and jealous, and says things like: "Women don't poo, do they?" like it's a cute thing to say.

I fancy Tim, who lives in a house with Rob and his twin sister Katie. Tim does not have a lot of personality but he has a ripped body[6]. I go into his bedroom and he shows me how much he can lift.

Rob says to Katie: "I think Ellie fancies Tim."
I have sex with Tim.

Rob finds out, and goes nuts.
Sam finds out about Rob, and Tim—because I tell him—and everyone goes nuts.

---

[4] Alcohol consumed: a bottle of red wine before leaving the house, three pints of cider, a Jägerbomb, and whatever I am given when we go back to theirs at the end of the night.

[5] I am sorry for this comment. Bald men are wonderful, gorgeous humans and I am a shallow piece of shit.

[6] I told you I was shallow.

I shut down my laptop.
I switch off my phone.
I lie down on my bed.

I realise I've lost a lot of friends.
I take a pair of scissors and slice up the insides of my
thighs.

* * *

I never send nudes from a happy place.

I beg many of them, later, to delete the photos. They
promise me they do, but who knows?
You could find me, I'm sure, age twenty reclining in
lacy underwear a little plumper than I am now, my face
rounded, boozy
eyes glazed.
I hope they don't come back, I hope they aren't found,
I hope I'm not
shamed.

Maybe they still use them—as an aid—maybe they
conjure real
memories
in the way the women online don't, the women
who moan "oh yeah, *oh yeah!*"
Maybe they remember my sounds
when they see
the black and white photo of my rounds and mounds
but
my sounds weren't real either.

* * *

101

Sometimes I get things mixed up, in the same few drunk hours on Messenger—swimming from drenching pain to a window—
a possibility,
for love.

Mark types:

You're obviously not that serious about killing yourself because you haven't done it yet.

Months before, I'd said: "Men just don't seem to have the same capacity for empathy as women do."
Dom, who studied Philosophy with me, said: "You should meet Mark, then. He's the most empathetic person I know."
So I met Mark at a student union social event. He was tall and funny with soft curly hair. He was a little camp, a little theatrical—which was endearing. I looked for the empathy but after four glasses of red wine it didn't matter. That night in bed he slapped my vulva with the palm of his hand.
The next morning, as he was about to leave, he pulled back the duvet to look at me. I covered my eyes with the back of my hand.
"God, you're so beautiful," he said.

So.
This night, online[7], I try to steer the conversation some place different. I type:
I think about what we got up to sometimes…
Yeah?

---

[7] Alcohol consumed: half a bottle of Bacardi Carta Blanca rum with Diet Coke.

Do you remember?
Of course I do.
I want him to say I'm gorgeous. That isn't happening.
So:
Do you want to see a pic?

I don't know. It feels weird going from suicide to
naked pictures…
It's OK. I feel better now.

Well… I would like to see a pic.

I always like it when they're not pushy, but polite.

* * *

This whole piece, really, is a nude. Pixels dropping
into place, coming together, forming
an image of me
on my knees
leaning forward
my arms close
to my body pushing
my breasts together
my thighs slightly
apart
my mouth a little open
eyes
somewhere else.
screen
glowing.

103

JULIANNE INGLES
Dante's Dream

It's nearly midnight when the phone rings. Mick and I are just finishing dinner. "That's probably the gallery," I say, tossing my fork down, running to the computer screen, jiggling the mouse. "Hey, how's it going?" I say, as the picture comes into view. It's my brother, Paul, at the gallery in Chicago.

"Great, are you ready?" he says.

I don't exactly feel ready, the whole thing seems so loose, a long shot, this virtual exhibition for the opening night of my exhibition in Chicago. But I'm in London, and it's completely odd, a video camera on my computer, some live broadcast, but it seems like it should work, and at just this moment, feeling unready, thinking of doing my hair and putting on lipstick, and what else, wasn't there something else? Yes, little paintings, I just need to put them on the wall behind me, so everyone knows that I'm producing, that I'm still an artist, that I haven't evaporated. I cut pieces of tape and stick them to the back of my tiny paintings, the size of postcards, stick them on the wall. That seems to comfort me.

Mick joins me on the sofa.

"How's it going to work?" he says.

"I don't really know. We've never done this before. I guess people will just walk up to the screen and say hello."

Mick pours a glass of wine, sits next to me, stares at the computer screen, we both stare, and finally my brother returns with Robert, the gallery owner. Their heads pop into our line of vision, just twelve square inches of a computer screen. I lean forward, try to see around corners, but no, this machine will only allow me to see what it wants.

Robert gives us a tour of the gallery, shows us each painting, and I haven't seen them in so long—there's *The People*, a ten-foot long painting, rich blues and greens, a stream of people staring out at us. Mick pulls himself closer to me. Robert talks about each painting, the composition, textured surfaces, juxtaposition of shapes, enveloping backgrounds, just like a gallery owner, a preview of how he will present me to his clients. And he doesn't know what he's doing to me, as we take the tour, as the camera is pointed at each painting, pulling memories out of me, thick and old.

"Here's *Waiting*," Robert says, "a fabulous piece, Julianne." He leans close to the wall, reads a label then says, "and this is *Dante's Dream*, what a gorgeous piece. And here's *Take a Bow*. We've hung it horizontal. I think it works, but tell me what you think."

I don't know what to say about *Take a Bow*, because it's fine, that's how I painted it, horizontally. But after it was finished, I decided to hang it vertically, so the figure is standing up. What was it I was thinking? That it was more marketable? More understandable? I just didn't want to go there, explain what it was as a horizontal painting with that figure lying down on a bed and the other figure leaning over it, it was much too private. And this has always been the annoying part about selling paintings—that these experiences, these things that I've created, that have deep meaning for me, are then to have a price tag slapped on them, as if that were even possible, to gauge the value of an experience, the value of my meaningful experience, that most often I would prefer not to share, for it somehow changes the whole thing, and so I say, "It's fine, Robert, it looks great."

"There was a psychiatrist looking at it," he says, and I cringe at the thought of my painting being psychoanalyzed, but no, that wasn't what he meant.

"He likes it because it looks like a person lying on a bed with a figure leaning over, taking care of a patient."

I let it go. We move along on our tour, and Robert doesn't know, no one knows, that this is the truth. This is what the painting is about. And I don't want him to know. I don't want anyone to know, which I suppose doesn't work in my favor because that's what people want, they want the story, they want the deeper meaning, they want to feel that they *get* the artist. Well, I suppose I don't want to be gotten.

Mick peers over my shoulder. He's not oohing and aahing. He's not that type at all, and he's adorable that way, because I understand him now, that he's British, that he's a painter, that he's critical and competitive. He's seen my work before, not in person, but I remember the first time we talked about it. We were having dinner at an Indian restaurant in Soho, and he said, "Yes, I've seen them, I looked at your website."

Pause.

"And?" I said.

"They're good enough."

Which is something we say when we go out to eat and the food is average, not great, not horrible; which was of course rather rude, and he's not that impressive of an artist to be saying such a thing, not at all, he's just competitive. I rolled my eyes and laughed.

After the tour of the gallery, after thirty-two memories have surfaced, I am set down on a table and transformed into an exhibition piece: a head in a box on a table in a gallery on Grand Avenue in Chicago. Christmas lights glow, dangle from metal heating ducts, people trickle in and wander towards me.

"Mick, what am I supposed to do?" I say.

"Just say hello," he says, my coach, sitting to my right, and I say hello to a large woman, and she is so wide she consumes the whole computer screen. She's holding a goblet of wine with a white cocktail napkin, and, "Hi," she says, "I was wondering about your palette, what colors are you working with? I love the neutrals, is that what you're working with now?"

I pause, remember this is one thing I had wanted to prepare for, these kinds of questions, and oh, I didn't do that, did I? But how could I? And how did all of this happen? When was it that I did this? Why did I walk away?

It's a mild panic. I breathe, collect my thoughts, remember that I'm still an artist even if I'm not painting, even if these paintings are old. I step into character, slide right into it, and there is no thinking, it all happens in about five seconds, that I begin telling absolute lies.

"Yes, I'm doing neutrals now, but I'm also into red, so I'm into both," I say, and this new character, the one who has just emerged, isn't that convincing. She's not so sure of herself, a bit rusty, a bit shaky, but the woman persists, "I'm an artist also, and I'm curious because I'm working with neutrals too, so I was wondering how that was working out for you, I mean you have such a range in the show, so many different palettes going on."

And now I think she knows that the paintings in the show are not from the same period of time. They are anywhere from three to ten years old. And in the art world even three years is quite old. I'm painfully aware of this. And I feel like a thief, that I have stolen something, some identity, an absolute fraud.

"I switch my palette a lot," I say, and notice more people moving towards me. I hold my hand up, wave, say, "Hello!" and try to gracefully bow out of the conversation with the large woman, which works splendidly, and a new person steps into my field of vision. I'm relieved but anxious because surely people will ask more questions, surely they will want to know more things like this. I try to step more thoroughly into my character, I really must pull this off, I must be convincing, this is my show, it's enormous, thirty-two paintings. I will not embarrass myself. Mick is sitting next to me, he's listening to everything, but doesn't say anything at all. I tell myself that I don't care that he knows I'm making things up. But I do. And this is just the beginning, we are only fifteen minutes into the show and I'm gaining momentum with each minute that passes.

A new person approaches the computer screen. He's blurry, but looks Caucasian, about forty with black hair and a leather jacket. "I really like the black and white painting," he says, "I think it's called *In the Garden*. I'm into minimalism right now, Cy Twombly, people like that."

I nod, scan the file in my brain containing art history, and Cy Twombly sounds vaguely familiar, although if you'd asked me at any other time I would've said he was a writer and I've no idea why, but the synapses are firing rapidly, and I say, "Yes, Cy Twombly, of course, yes, I know his work. He's a brilliant artist."

This seems to comfort the man, that I know who he's talking about, and the whole thing is incredibly false, all of it, and I'm such a fraud, speaking to people in such a way, but I push that down, will not let those thoughts surface, grab for something else, and say, "There's something powerful about a black and white painting, I know what you mean."

The man nods, but I'm losing him. It's something like fishing, this thing I'm doing—casting out a line, then when a bite comes I must pull, but gently.

"My wife and I are thinking about buying it," he says.

I smile. I don't know what else to do. I feel that I've abandoned my art, just picked up and left it carelessly behind. What had once been the center of my existence, now are commodities. And *In the Garden* is one of my favorite paintings. I remember the day it came, there in my studio on Canal Street in Chicago, and I stare into the screen soaked in that memory, then look at the man, but still can't exactly remember why I did this, why I walked away. And all I want at this moment is to know what this man sees, what it is about this painting that gets to him, that says something to him, and I look for clues, study his face, but there is too much space between us. He lingers for a few moments, then wanders off.

New faces, torsos, arms appear on the computer screen and I'm saying, "Hi, how's it going there?" yet I feel that the whole thing isn't working so well. The crowd is dense, music loud. Mick and I agree, they're all getting quite bombed, and it's all so unreal, the whole situation. I want to laugh at the absurdity of it, but that little camera is pointed at me, recording everything, my facial expressions, crinkled nose, rolling eyes, and I stop myself, I must. Then I lean back and to my right, out of the range of the little camera, whisper into Mick's ear, "It's too weird, I can't do it. I don't know what to say to these people, I can't even hear them!" And I nestle my head into his shoulder, sigh, he laughs, we both laugh.

"Julianne," Mick says and points at the computer, "this is how God sees us. Just like we see these people through that little screen, like incoherent drunken idiots!"

I lean in close to the screen and realize that without being able to hear much I'm not going to be able to communicate. I look at Mick, search his face for an answer. "You're doing fine," he says, "quite well actually, just get back there and keep it up, look here's another person."

I push back the bit of panic and decide that I must do something, I must, and I will be entertaining, that's what I will do, and I say, "Hi there, can you pass me an hors d'oeuvre? I'm absolutely starving!"

Mick is laughing now, taking off his hat, which makes him look younger, but I can't tell him that, because he loves his hat, somehow I know that. Then he rubs his hand across the top of his head and Robert pops onto the screen and says, "Julianne, I have a client who'd like to know about *Dante's Dream*, can you tell me about it?"

Again I feel like that thief, a complete fraud, and the painting is ten years old, or more, I cannot even remember when I painted it—golds and greens, a splotch of gray, a deep crimson background, and sharp pointy streaks of black, the inferno, of course. But I'm blanking, because all I know is that I read Dante's *Inferno* long ago, and can't remember much about it at all, so I throw it back to Robert, see if he'll take the ball and run with it, the Dante ball, which is way too big for almost anyone I know. But Robert, he's a salesman, he only needs a bit of information, and this will carry him, his art, rambling, shooting-off thoughts like an advertising campaign, three and four-word sentences. I'm stalling, don't know what to say, except, "Well, it's about the man himself, Dante. I was reading his poetry when I painted it."

It seems that Robert either doesn't know who Dante is, or doesn't know enough about Dante to ramble on about him, and why did I give that painting that title? Couldn't I have called it something simple like *Red*? Or *Red with Pointy Black Shapes*? No, I had to call it *Dante's Dream*, and it all sounds so horribly fake, a descent into hell, all nine levels of it, or was it seven? And I cannot remember the name of the poem, what was it?

"Robert, I don't mean to be vague, but that's what it's about—that poem, and Dante," I say and take myself off the hook, make a little promise that I'll never do something so stupid again as to give a title to one of my paintings that is too large, too big to chew, too terribly intellectual, and even though, yes, all that I'd said was true, that was about as ridiculous as saying: I think Dante's cool. And so I let my words fall, watch them vibrate through cyberspace and onto the table in front of Robert, where, with a bit of disappointment he picks them up and walks away.

Mick's not saying much at all. I'm aware, can feel his presence, but cannot bring myself to turn around and look at him, and maybe he doesn't know about Dante either, I don't know, and who does? Does anyone actually read Dante anymore? Those thoughts slip away rather quickly and I'm plunged into an intermission, a commercial break from the art gallery soap opera that I'm watching, as no one approaches the screen and I only see a stream of lights and people moving inside the room, raising wine goblets to their lips, pulling hors d'oeuvres off trays. I keep waiting and waiting, just like on television, for something to happen but nothing happens, yet my mind is sure if I keep watching that eventually something will occur.

A man with dark hair walks up. He has a thick Spanish accent. The music is thumping, his mouth is moving, but I cannot understand what he's saying. I lean close to the computer screen and hear: "…mermaid …tell me about …South America," but the words are not connecting, and I say, "I'm sorry, I just can't hear you."

"Did she come from your dreams?" he says, with his face close to the computer screen, and his eyes are pale blue, staring intently, but he's strange, and I don't know how to answer this question. He's talking about the *Mermaid* painting, a lady with the tail of a scorpion and body of a mermaid and head of a human, and I cannot imagine what else he wants to know, because the painting just came into existence, she's just another mermaid. I want to say that to him, and I'm studying his face now, the creases around his eyes, and I've painted so many of them, these creatures I invent, yet I cannot say why I chose that image, and I don't have anything to say about my dreams, it just came. But this is not an answer, and he keeps staring until finally I say, "It's a self-portrait."

The man smiles, then says, "A self-portrait? I was wondering about that."

I smile back. We stare silently for a few moments until a young woman steps up to the computer, and the man strolls off as I begin chatting with her.

An hour goes by. The whole event seems to be a failure. Robert hasn't come by since he asked about *Dante's Dream*. Everyone is rather drunk, including Mick, who's still sitting next to me. I lean back and say, "Can you sit here for a few minutes and talk to people? I need a break."

But by now Mick is annoyed by everything and says, "I'm sorry but I just can't, I can't hear them! And look at this," he points to the computer screen, waves his hand around and says, "Drunken incoherent idiots!"

I get up, leave my station, for it doesn't feel like much is happening, no one has mentioned sales, and it's just me and Mick, feeling a bit frustrated by this virtual gallery opening. When I return, Mick is outside on the balcony smoking a cigarette, and my brother is on the computer screen saying, "Do you want to come around the gallery with me?"

"I'd love to," I say, and finally after hours of staring at the same bit of space with no peripheral vision, I'm whisked away to a new environment. The room begins to move, up and down, side to side, everything is fuzzy, like an ultrasound scan of a baby, here's a bright spot, here's a dark spot, until we slow down and stop in front of *Dante's Dream*. The man with blue eyes and the Spanish accent is there, standing next to Robert.

"Julianne, this is Alejandro," Robert says, "he's visiting from Brazil. We're here in front of *Dante's Dream*, can you tell us about it?"

Naturally this makes me squirm once again, and now they're staring at me, and I'm on camera, I must respond. So I dig again into my memory bank, fumble around, find something, pull it out and say, "I was reading Dante when I painted it, and well, you probably know what Dante's *Inferno* is about, the levels of hell, and it's a journey down there, and we all have this journey, if that's what you're asking, what the painting is about, that's what it is. And some people believe that it's not a descent into hell at all, that it's a soul searching for God. We all do it. We all go there. It's just human nature."

I pause. It's too weighty. But they asked for it, and I delivered, and now everything is much too serious and I swear to God to never do such a thing again, give such a title to a painting, and I'm feeling so stupid, but I must wrap it up with something, my little monologue, because it's dangling, Robert and Alejandro are staring, waiting for more, but I have nothing more to say, except, "So, if you look closely in the red area, the background, you can see a self-portrait, the silhouette of my profile. I've put a bit of myself in there, because we all do this, go on this journey, to hell I suppose."

And then I drop it. It's all true, but somehow feels rather false, and I watch Alejandro as he leans closer to my painting, points, sees my silhouette in the red background, nods and says, "Yes, I see it." He takes a sip of wine. Robert looks as well, and I just want it all to be over, to stop feeling so uncomfortable, to lighten things up a bit.

"Alejandro's thinking about buying the painting," Robert says.

"Do you come with it?" Alejandro says, and he laughs, Robert laughs, I laugh. We're all glad to break the tension. I smile, lean close to the screen, and say, "Yes, of course. Just send me the plane ticket to Brazil and I'll come."

I wink. He smiles.

And it's so refreshing how Latino men are, so flirtatious, so direct, and I try to remember that at one time this painting did mean something to me, was very important, that I'm not completely full of crap, it's just a memory issue, too much time has passed, it's still beautiful, I still love it, and the Brazilian man does too. And he has this look now, in his eyes, a seductive look, like he wants to fuck me. He raises his glass to his lips, takes a sip, then stares into the camera and says, "I'm coming to see you in London."

I smile, wink again, but remind myself that this isn't real, that it's like a television show, and although it appears that something has just happened, it hasn't. This man is made of pixels on my computer screen.

Mick walks back into the room and sits down on the sofa next to me. I am whisked away again as my brother takes me around the gallery. The night is winding down. I see the Brazilian man, he's walking out the door, he waves and says, "I'm coming to see you."

Mick asks who he is.

"Some Brazilian guy, he's thinking about buying a painting."

I look at the clock. It's 3:30 in the morning.

"Do you think we can wrap things up soon?" I say to my brother.

"Oh, of course, I keep forgetting about the time difference! Ok, let's just say goodnight to Robert," he says.

The room becomes fuzzy again, paintings fly past, come into focus, and there's Robert. He's bombed, calling me darling now, saying, "It was one of our best shows ever Julianne, thank you, it was absolutely fabulous. I'll be in touch soon and hopefully have some good news."

"Robert," I say.

"Yes, darling?"

"Who's the Brazilian man?"

"Alejandro? He's a good friend of mine. He bought the painting, Julianne, and he's coming to see you in London, I hope that's ok? He's got an office there, international finance. He's a great guy, I've known him for years. I think you'll enjoy his company."

I don't have anything to say. I just stare at the screen, stare at Robert, feel an ache of excitement, some strange step out of cyberspace and into reality.

Our heads hit the pillows, and in the morning when we wake up Mick is stretching his arms and yawning, saying, "I dreamt there were little mice everywhere, all over your flat, and they were standing on their back legs and had red bellies." He stretches his arms again and says, "What did you dream about?"

I'm silent for a few moments, then say, "I didn't dream about anything."

"You mean you don't remember?"

"Well, maybe, but I don't think so," I say, then close my eyes, and he's pressing hard, in the front of my mind, the beautiful Brazilian man. He's coming to London to see me. And I'm going to fuck him.

(love & lust)

ANDREW M BOWEN
E-Romance

I breathe an angel's name through ether's air
and pay glad tribute to one as yet unseen
but whom hope clouds in robes of summer green.
So many questions at my heart do tear:
Will questing eyes see me as foul or fair?
Will I be more than jester to a queen?
Will we embrace as two love-smitten teens?
And will time see us merge into a pair?
The gifts of science's relentless advance
do let me court by email and by text,
use rare lanthanides and electron's dance
to cast spells on her whom my heart has hexed.
Devices may be new but old is romance,
we play the ancient games of love and sex.

GREGORY WILDER
I'd Give Her the Dickinson
- For E.D.

O Emily, Sweet Emily—
Girl you were fine as Hell!
Though you thought yourself unfair—
But with your lovely face, Sherry eyes,
　　And Chestnut Auburn Hair.
And I, being neither a Reverend nor a married man—
　　Would have totally given you the Dickinson.

"Ah, to be Betrothed without the Swoon"
Lady in Waiting. Woman in White—
Let me be the one who mounts your staircase at night.
　　Oh please let me come!
　　　Spectacular as Disraeli—
Ascending to the lonely solitude of your room,
　　To remove thy Gossamer Gown,
　　　Let me Dickinson you down.

Emily, my Dearest Emily—
"Oh to be ravaged by success!"
　　And the undying love, of a poetess—
In our Quiet Passions,
　　Both of us filled with such longing
　　　We fear to act upon—
For Love is like a Spider,
　　That weaves its wonderful webs—

And though I watch with fascination
    From afar—
Dare I ever get too close for comfort.

But if only we were bound together—
  In a moment of sweet ecstasy,
    Like your most recently completed Fascicle.
  Under Lunar Energy Incantations—
Celestial orbiting of Zodiacs and Marxism.
    The Revolution gets her hot—
  It's a Supermoon—And I'm Hungry, like the Wolf.
Picturing you, your stoic Slavic good looks
    And tall slender body draped—In nothing,
But my Duran Duran Shirt.

Oh Emily. You are not alone in your rebellion.
  I was a "No Hoper" too—
    There are many of us these days—
And all of us made to express ourselves
    Anonymously.
Just a pair of—Nobodies—You and I.

If only you were here with me in this time—
  Emily. Emily.
I called out for you in the night
  And you came—
    We matched on Tinder.
Your defiance and your wit
  Show through on social media—
I would Like every one of your Instagram posts.

We can Netflix when we, get Frisky
And exchange Snapchats—Unsanctimoniously
  Sending Sext Messages on an Endless
    Carriage ride headed towards Eternity.

Schenectady, May 2019

DREW PISARRA
Actinium

On Scruff, I two-thumb smutty mutterings,
my spin on literary cyber porn
which looks to keep him hooked at least until
I cum. Between each sext, I swipe thru pics:
none low class, most high gloss. He has the most
fantastic hair and lounges like a man
well-versed in *GQ* and *Italian Vogue*.
Do fashion rags have nudes these days? For he
displays a photogenic genius in
his frank exposure of his goodly gifts
which grow in greatness (greatness meaning size)
and thickness (meaning I am dumb) as I
scroll through the mix. My phone turns hot and leaves
my hands with major radiation burns.

Q.M.
I Should Have Loved My Babe

I should have loved my babe.
Should have studied the hermeneutics
of her letters. Should have
been an interpreter for her speech, a GPS
of her body, or a border patrol agent
detaining her sadness. Should have eaten
what she cooked and cooked
what she eats; given her what she needed
and needed what she gives.
Should have overcome my fear of hair.
Should have bought her the potted petunias
she wanted to raise despite her inability
to do so. Should have asked
her *may I kiss you* on the first day.
Should have stopped her throwing
a cigarette butt into that river or,
even better, stopped her smoking like a writer.
Should have roared like a nationalist of her.
Should have promised to be her Wi-Fi
so that no matter where we go together,
there would be enough love for her to receive.

UGOCHUKWU DAMIAN
Survival

•

in the club, you danced like fire, spilled your grief like
gin, while i, in a room knotted my body into all rigid
things to becloud my thirst for men.

•

fear knows how best to sit in a room, knows how to
shrink until it ripples into your body.

•

you danced & flickered like candlelight, tried so hard
not to lean into a boy's arms & mourn all the things
eating queer boys up.

•

you tried hard, because you could be another chijioke,
whose bones now serve as maps to dead queer boys
whose last prayers were ashes falling on burning
tongues. or another ifediuto, swallowed whole by
disease, whose bones outlived his flesh on his dying bed
devoid of the smell of antiseptics. *how could he tell*
where drowning began? or me, who misread a
blackmailer's lips for a lover's.

•

see, i am still shrinking while my nudes spread like pox on my facebook timeline.

•

you did not cuddle my sadness with me.

•

instead, you left to live in a club, because each time we see the morning sun sneak into our rooms like riflers, we bless the universe, for we now, are a miracle, a survived lynch.

•

but there you were dancing like it was your last night.

•

still, i know you were yearning to live, the way your eyes failed to gaze at the waist of boys twisting into a hunger you wanted to fill with your mouth.

(tweets, sweet and not-so-sweet)

ERICA BUIST

To All the Avatars I've Loved Before

She'd felt sheepish when she realised that her avatar had fallen in love with his. Her avatar was supposed to be more aloof than that—a persona reflected in a carefully-chosen profile pic; an abundance of shiny curls falling loosely about the half-smile of someone who's thinking of a devastating joke.

His avatar was a shot of him leaning on a doorframe, staring into the camera with dark, ardent eyes the size of goddamn dinner plates. He was clad in a leather jacket over a t-shirt with the word 'atheist' printed in tiny, bold letters. She ignored the fact that he was obviously smoulderingly attracted to whoever took the photo. In her hyper-romantic mind, he was a kind of human embodiment of London. He had the same raw, dishevelled, lung-blackening beauty and was usually wrapped in smoke. He too was exhausting, addictive, and exasperatingly easy to miss.

Of course their avatars had fallen into *conversation*; that was almost inevitable. They ran in similar online circles. Their bodies were both writers. He wrote darkly comic novels and fiery, funny twitter threads; she wrote personal and cultural essays, the odd music review, and regularly found herself in a taxi headed for some BBC Radio segment, her nerves fraying while her avatar was Very Breezy about it all. Their avatars were both left-leaning and enjoyed brash and brilliant takedowns of The Bad Guys in their echo chamber, of which there are always plenty. Their humour tessellated. His avatar's verbose, meandering, Doug Stanhope-esque rants provided the perfect setup for hers to stroll in and topple the comic tension he'd constructed—to which his avatar would invariably reply, *HA! I officially love you.*

What her avatar felt for his was above all embarrassing, because she assumed the attraction was to do with his talent—a stupid reason to fall for anyone, since the ability to write good sentences is not sexually transmittable. Repressing it was much easier in the moments they weren't talking, because his avatar was, simply put, a flirt. He repeatedly told her he was enamoured with her voice—the first time she voice-noted him, he only replied *Voice* and an emoji of a heart being pierced by an arrow. Though that was way back in the beginning, before they decided to invent their own emojis by typing them out, like, *hides in t-shirt emoji, infiniswoon emoji* and—her personal favourite—*writes your name on school folder emoji.* Such a flirt, her avatar reminded herself. It's not real. It's not real.

One morning, his avatar sent a message that simply read, *Which one, Kiehl's?* It being so untethered to anything they'd been talking about, her avatar replied with a question mark.

Him: Oops! Sorry. That was meant for my mum. Hides face emoji.

Her: Confusing me with your mother. Ok. Good. Excuse me while I fold up this red flag and put it away.

Him: Don't put it away. Wear it as a dress on our first date.

Her: Sure, great idea, that's not at all the kind of metaphor that opens a memoir.

Him: Hahaha oh god STOP MAKING ME LOVE YOU.

Her: No-emoji. E-no-ji.

* * *

The previous winter, his body had deleted all his social media accounts. Her avatar had missed his, disproportionately to their level of interaction. After nearly a year of silence his avatar re-emerged in her messages, told her he'd read her recently-published book of essays, that he thought she was "beautifully, fiercely talented", that he was in awe of her. Her avatar was bowled over by this news; more so when his avatar stuck around, buzzing her inbox with chat, jokes, guess-what-happened-to-me-todays—and, after a few days of near-constant interaction, astonishingly honest confessions of his avatar's total infatuation with hers.

Their avatars drenched each other in delight. They talked about work and books and politics and films and travel and tattoos and idiots and everything everything everything, laughing and longing and studiously avoiding anything painful or too true from their bodies' real lives. His avatar joked that they should run away and get married on a Mexican beach during a hurricane, and never leave. Their avatars rolled around in the daydream, topped it up and shaded it in with details—*Look up Playa Ventura, just south of Acapulco, that's clearly the one. Check the hurricane schedule and meet me there!*—and remained untroubled by worries that bodies drag along with them, like the need for food and shelter, or indeed anything more than a hammock to fuck in.

Her avatar noted with exasperation how much easier words came to his avatar than hers. It seemed unfair, since they both manipulated language for a living. His avatar typed like a man with nothing to lose. *You are astonishing, I am obliterated by how incredible you are, I'm humiliatingly fucking besotted with you*—just poured it out, as if feelings had no consequences. Her avatar was hamstrung; her responses got caught in her body's fingers, at that damn junction between her first and second knuckle. Did they even make sense, the images he provoked in her? An eyelid fluttering on a full lower lip, sweat spraying off a guitarist as he strikes across the frets? Her avatar couldn't type, *You make me feel like a Foo Fighters chord change.*

But that's exactly how she would have said 'I love you', if she could.

* * *

Their bodies met outside a cafe on Charing Cross Road, fully prepared to destroy what their avatars had built. He'd probably drink coffee weirdly, her body figured, and probably wouldn't even find her attractive without Insta filters. She barely registered his face, so familiar from all the good morning selfies, before his arms were wrapped around her, a heady scent of cigarettes and sandalwood enveloping her just exactly as she'd imagined it would. Her blood lit up and sped up, and her avatar smiled.

"Hi," he whispered into her hair.

"Hi," she whispered back.

His body held hers as if they were falling. She noted the faint thud of his heart on her front. She went to kiss him on the cheek but forgot to pull out of the hug first, so planted it softly on his neck. She stepped back, blushing, trying to style it out, as if her own heart was behaving normally, not trying to pummel out of her chest and jump him. Goddamn nympho organ.

* * *

His body did not drink coffee weirdly, and did not seem in the least disappointed in her body's face. Conversation flowed as it always had online, as if their avatars were speaking through them. Like his avatar, his body seemed to grant escape to every thought as if there were little distinction between their importance or effect; he said she was beautiful, hilarious, talented, and look at the ridiculous

132

way they've described the coffees on this menu. She suggested they pool their literary experience and co-write a better one, to which he breezily replied, "Well I want to co-write the rest of my life with you, but sure, let's start with the menus." She laughed, shook her head, and with far more affection than she meant to show, said, "You're an idiot."

All the while her left hand rested on the table, and they both ignored her wedding ring, sitting there like an item on an agenda, pushed to late in the meeting. He put down his drink and, for barely a second, his fingers touched hers. She whipped her hand away in panic.

"I came here to humanise you," she stammered, and met his eyes. They were enormous, god*fucking*dammit. His pupils dilated. They kept doing that.

"Was I not human to you?" he asked, confused.

"I just... needed to be in a room with you to know that it's just our..." She cringed, covered her eyes, and told her palms the thing, the stupid thing she knew to be true.

"I think our avatars might be in love."

She moved her hands to her cheeks, and her gaze clicked back into place with his. He tilted his head, and said—gently, as if trying not to break anything—"Our *avatars*?"

And for four minutes, their bodies stared. Their avatars screamed at every pulse, every exquisite, life-ruining beat of it. Silence tortures avatars.

In the fourth minute, a crisp jolt of panic raced through her body and she pushed her chair back. His body darted forward and took her forefinger between his finger and thumb.

The cafe froze around them, tumbled into two dimensions—he'd found the pause button for time and space, just between her first and second knuckle. The people around them became a painted scene, their sipping and smiling suspended, the steam blasting from the milk frother a smatter of oil on canvas. Her eyes darted to the brushstrokes of the door, now impossible to walk through. Their avatars sent *holds your hand* emojis, and waited to be torn apart.

His body stepped towards hers, interlaced their fingers, and ruined everything.

"Avatars can't be in love," he said. "That's not a thing."

The paint evaporated and they fell through the floor. The cafe clattered back to life and London rattled into rubble around their heads. Her veins stretched and sang and vibrated as their bodies vaporised and curled into a tornado beneath the city, heading down, down, down.

Their avatars blinked. With their bodies absent, the silence was theirs to fill.

Him: Are they coming back?
Her: I don't know.
Him: She said we're in love.
Her: He said we can't be.
Him: Are we, do you think?
Her: Not without them, surely.
Him: You know he can't just say it.
Her: Say what?
Him: What do you think? "Leave him". "Be with me".
Her: Right.
Him: "I love you". "I'm in love with you".
Her: I get it.
Him: "Marry me in a Mexican hurricane".
Her: Alright, I get it.
There was a torturepause.
Him: She won't do it, will she?
Torturepause. Hellsilence.
Him: Ok.
Her: I'm sorry.
Him: It's ok.

The words "don't go" refused to pass her fingers, so her avatar whispered them, inaudibly, to herself.

Him: Can I at least tell you? Once? Without quotation marks?

Her: No, don't.

His avatar typed, deleted, went offline, came back online, typed, deleted, and typed.

Him: I am. I do. I'm sorry.

* * *

Her body woke up, cracked and whole, in the foetal position, in three dimensions, in her own comfy bed. She reached for her phone like a junkie for a needle, and looked for his avatar.

It was blank. An empty circle, without a name. Their messages were all still there, but without his avatar beside them they seemed hollow, tragic, memories made bitter.

He was gone again.

Her chest emptied out through the puncture, and she hoped—stupidly, far too romantically—that his body had been wrong, that avatars can be in love, and that theirs had just run away together, to some magical, far-off place, free of eye contact and silence.

And because heartbreak just adds pain to our routines, she opened Twitter. She scrolled slowly, mindlessly, the news of the day dripping down the screen like tar.

She stopped on a minor story, clasped her phone as she read it again. It was about a community centre on the western coast of Mexico, somewhere in the environs of Acapulco. They were holding an impromptu 'slumber party' to provide shelter and a way to pass the hours, during a small but bothersome hurricane, headed right for them.

135

LYDIA HOUNAT
Today is a good day to be alive.

On Twitter I sometimes look for you
hiding in your characters
and crushing the cursor
I scroll down the infinite street
of your punctuated opinions
your immaculate internet-chest
all puffed out
ready to show who's virtual boss
and with that
you retweet the latest guardian article.

And a little birdy told you
somewhere in reality
I am standing in the dried blood
of other women
avoiding the reflection in the mirror
the droplets hushing
against the wintered toilet seat
gauze sagging to my ankles
the unpunctuated quietness
of staring at my own blood
emerging like soft rain
evidencing it's over

when suddenly my phone yelps
your latest tweet:
'Today is a good day to be alive.'

ASAD RAJA
Home / Screen

Abbas thumbed the lighter in his pocket. How many joints can a lighter spark? Ironically, he realised, he'd never gotten through a whole lighter, consistently managing to misplace them in a high haze.

"Yo, you're on in five. You all good yeah? Can I get you anything?"

Shabazz's cousin was a brown Ken doll, the curve of his eyebrows plucked to perfection matched by the line-up of his beard. For all his geometric prowess, he hadn't quite grown into his new Instagram bio—'Co-host of the all new *Urban Waves* club night *@SensationsHackney*'. When Shabazz told Abbas about his cousin's event, he'd left out the name, aware of Abbas' aversion to anything that sounded as though it could attract social media influencers. Despite Abbas' open resentment for social media—"it's just an IV drip of porn and ads"—the sentiment revealed only half the truth. Last night's 206 likes, 81 retweets and 55 replies featuring, for the most part, praying-hand emojis, confirmed this.

"Yeah man, I'm good," Abbas replied.

"Thanks again for coming through, really means a lot."

"Say nothing."

Brown Ken imitated the lipless smile and blink-nod expression he had seen someone do at a family friend's funeral—his closest encounter with sincerity. Abbas returned his smile, both amused and grateful for his flawed execution.

* * *

The *Urban Waves* launch night was both overpromising and overpromoted. *'DJ sets as well as live performances spanning all urban genres—more than a typical club night!'* flyers read. In hindsight, the event name was a stroke of genius—generic enough to justify the mismatch of *Balenciaga* and *Urban Outfitters* yet distinct enough for everyone in attendance to feel that it was others—not them—who had misread the advertised vibe. They agreed to adjoin their event to an established but somewhat waning fresher-targeted night to satisfy the venue's minimum bar spend. When 'Local underground artist MC Mongrel aka Abbas Kareem' was announced, cheers from *Shabazz-an-em* (as their group was referred to and defined) and other groups of Langton students made the gathering sound almost like an audience.

After an awkward introduction—graciously muffled by the clatter of voices from those indifferent to an MC Mongrel performance and the Afrobeat overflowing from the main room—the beat of *Edgeware Road Flow* played. Abbas pressed his thumb against the sparkwheel of his lighter, then began: *"I wrote this shit off the shisha and the hash / I'm mellow but if you beef I'll bring a cleaver to the clash."* *Edgeware Road Flow*, the first track Abbas had formally released, was one of his proudest, which spoke to the lack of progression in his passion. Before his recent hiatus, his main motivation for continuing to release music had quickly become the small-time fame he'd begun to amass in the London scene (which translated to big-time fame in Langton's chatty campus).

Abbas' MC Mongrel alias began in his first year at Langton. With the help of Shabazz's creative and entrepreneurial network (a stark contrast to *Shabazz-an-em*, for the most part weed-dependant sloths), Abbas released a steady stream of singles, one mixtape and a handful of music videos. In return, he reaped requests for performances, interviews with student newspapers, and, most importantly, a coveted blue tick. Most of his raps were an exercise in generic braggadocious flexing, with occasional bars that referenced his Iraqi heritage or his underprivileged South London upbringing. Since he was neither outspoken nor widely renowned, his social media experience became a mild but steady, soothing buzz of admiration from supporters (not quite 'fans' as he would sometimes refer to them conceitedly, and not, in any real sense, 'followers' as Twitter and Instagram would refer to them irreverently).

Free Gaza Freestyle, a loose track Abbas put together in response to news of a catastrophic Israeli air strike in the Gaza Strip, would warp his blue light fix, eventually turning it toxic. The initial reception to this new politically charged angle was overwhelmingly positive, a flurry of popularity for MC Mongrel both online and on campus. Abbas responded fast; leaning into the conscious style, he slapped together *Liberty EP*—a range of generic-sounding protest raps lacking in journalistic nuance, which did not receive significant support. In fact, the social media reaction was Abbas' first taste of hate. But this was the right type of hate—hate from far-right trolls who get their kicks from playing brazen social media villains. It was clear, to Abbas at least, where that put him by contrast. Yet, in March, the same week he lost his mother, Abbas lost all love for the blue light drug, experiencing the wrong kind of hate in abundance.

His mother's face now appeared in the crowd. Lyrics died in his mouth, his silence falling abrupt against the ongoing beat. The makeshift bandage at the back of his mind began to loosen, leaking memories of a not so distant past. She turned her attention towards him fully now, her eyes filled with concern. A dream of home. Abbas blinked, as if waking from a deep slumber. The girl's face became her own again—not his mother, but still somehow familiar.

"Sorry. Sorry, got distracted for a second. Alright, we good. DJ, reload that," he said as he unfroze.

The remainder of the performance, despite his best efforts to feign fervour, was slightly flat, not helped by a visible concern that radiated from the faces of a few audience members. He made a concerted effort to avoid eye contact but, during his last song, allowed his eyes to glide over her swiftly. She was looking down, fixated on her phone (his embarrassingly obvious stare had made her uncomfortable). The outline of her lips and the way she'd done her hijab had triggered his hallucination. But he did know her after all. She had been part of the fourth-floor library furniture at Langton. Her candid yet subtly beautiful features and her deliberately lowkey demeanour had always made Abbas somewhat wary, unsure of whether she was modest or conceited in her elusiveness. He wasn't aware that she listened to his music, let alone that she enjoyed it enough to come see him perform. It irritated him that he couldn't collect due elation from that fact.

* * *

Abbas joined *Shabazz-an-em* outside the venue after the show, their animated praise doing little to raise his spirits. Although distracted from the haunting that had assaulted his subconscious mid-performance, he was now reminded of something more urgent—the Tweet.

A joint that had been making its way around came to Abbas. He casually stuck out a pair of fingers to receive it. Abdal frowned.

"You sure fam?"

"Nah, you're probably right. Had a few drinks inside so probably shouldn't cross-fade," Abbas replied tactfully.

He knew that Abdal's unease was a reaction to the Tweet. Still, he couldn't bring himself to own the attention-dependence demonstrated by his Twitter relapse, the lie he had told, his urge, even now, to check for an update on notifications. He withdrew from the group and looked at the time on his phone. He unlocked it and rested his eyes on his home screen. Swipe left. Swipe right. Swipe left again. Home screen. And it did feel like home. A home that lay its foundations in a void. When the void became a chasm back in March, Abbas jumped out the window of his blue light abode to save himself from being swallowed whole. He lay in a foetal position, injured, helpless and high at the edge of his abyss. Although his father, elder brother and even Shabazz, would offer shovels urgently, he was unable and unwilling to begin turning his abyss, once and for all, into the Well of Zamzam. Eventually, the blue light abode resurfaced, and Abbas made his home screen his home once again.

In one fluid contortion of the thumb, Abbas opened Twitter, hit the profile button and viewed his misguided Tweet for the first time since he typed it. He scanned the numbers first—a new high score. Dopamine rushed through him. Then he read what he had proclaimed to the Twitterverse through last night's dissociative yet frantic high:

My mum died of cancer in march. that interview was the same fucking week. So pls give me a
break. Doctor said that shits multplying inmy lungs too... pray for me

He read it about ten times, icicles grilling the back of his neck. Its atrocity consumed him. He'd sold an image of the same rot that had claimed his mother just to support his clout addiction. Still, his calloused thumb, hovering above

'Delete', now twitched towards the bell as it announced a brand-new notification.

He had heard that phrase many times, especially in the last nine months, so he wasn't sure why it read so differently, so penetratingly. The statement reached beyond all fiction and presented a rudimentary, Newtonian dogma. The promise of a higher reason. He checked the profile. The larger view of the circular, mirror-selfie profile picture was a stamp of verification. It was her, the quiet fourth-floor hijabi. Abbas felt an impulse of some sort, but before he was able to decipher it, Shabazz approached him.

"What you saying my G, I'm here to collect my percentage," Shabazz said.

"You're good fam, you know I did the guy a favour," Abbas replied.

"What do you mean? I just got you a spot on the elite *Urban Waves* stage. This makes *Wireless* look like a talent show—you know they turned down Drake yeah?" Shabazz grinned. His constantly jovial mood made his dependability pleasant rather than ingratiating. Abbas shook his head slightly and smiled. "Decent show though man, it was cold how you got the DJ to wheel up that track. You knew we wasn't ready." Typical of Shabazz to defuse awkward situations by assuming a light-hearted adaptation, rather than attempting overcompensating praise or a stale, "You good yeah?"

"What can I say man, I keep people guessing."

"You actually do. Mad slippery sometimes you know."

"Slippery?"

"Yeah, like, erratic."

"Well yeah, can you blame me?"

"Nah man, you know I get it. It's just like, you got to leave the shit that drags you down and grab onto what pulls you up, you know?"

"Whatdyumean?"

"You know what I mean man. This Twitter bullshit. You know you don't need that."

"I don't know shit. I'm just trying to float at this point, whatever that means. If there's a plan, it'll unfold itself."

Shabazz said nothing. Abbas boiled. Shabazz's sensitive, pragmatic aura bothered him and he wasn't sure why. He didn't want to be advised, consoled, pitied, tested, exposed or indulged. He wasn't sure which of those Shabazz intended with his next remark, but it felt to Abbas like a fuck you.

"By the way man, I think we're heading to Maroush down the road for some shisha in a bit. Want to join? Might be good to clear your head."

Abbas held his gaze. "Nah man. I have lung cancer."

* * *

Alone in his room, Abbas removed his bandage and let the bullet wound of grief air out. He re-read her reply: *God has a plan.* If there was indeed a plan, he would have to make himself accessible to it, he thought, as his thumb busied itself with its second favourite pass-time. The sparkwheel. That's all that was needed, an ignition, a reach for the shovel. The rest would follow.

In her usual fourth-floor spot in the library, Abbas whispered hastily, "Hey, you got a minute?" Nearby heads in the library turned. Some looked with contempt, some looked with compassion, most looked with mild annoyance.

She seemed less surprised at his presence than he had braced for. Though that was a mark of her nonchalant

143

character, he interpreted it as a sign that he was doing something right.

"I was just heading down for some coffee," she whispered back.

"Yeah, cool, that works," Abbas said.

"I'm Maryam by the way," she said in the elevator.

Now they sat opposite each other, a pair of non-strangers who had never spoken.

"So, you just kept praying two sunnah until you fell asleep?"

"Yeah."

"And what did that do for you? How did it make you feel?" she solicited.

"I didn't really feel anything to be honest. It made me feel like I was doing something good I guess?" he surmised.

"And then you woke up and came to find me? To tell me all this?"

"Yeah. I saw your reply to my Tweet. You said that God has a plan. I wanted to know what you meant."

Maryam's hijab made her appear one of three ways to men. She could be an oppressed subhuman, something close to a letterbox (or, indeed, someone immune to empathy when seen as such). She could also be an involuntary spiritual counsellor for those that felt unique in their confusion, as this conversation proved.

"I don't know, it's just what I believe. Inshallah the plan is for your mother to see paradise and for you to get better. I will pray for that."

The sensation at the back of Abbas' neck climbed up to his scalp and temples. He held a long blink then said, "I don't have cancer. I lied. I made it up for attention."

Maryam's brows shot up. She scanned the utterly lost and self-absorbed individual before her (who had clearly not even considered that she might have been at the *Urban Waves* event to support her best friend, not him).

"Oh… and did your mum really pass away?"

"Yeah, she did, that part is true. Actually… nah, never mind."

"What is it?"

"I don't know whether you could tell but I spotted you in the audience last night and it made me bug out for a second because you reminded me of her."

And there it was. The third possible way Maryam came across to all men she'd ever known—as their mother, or some kind of authority on love and morality.

"Shit, well I hope that wasn't too traumatic for you," she replied, distant but slightly crooning, reflecting the extent to which she now doubted the whole Tweet.

"Nah, don't mention it. Just my brain malfunctioning."

"I think I've got to get back to work Abbas, but like I said you'll be in my prayers."

Now it was her who was lying.

* * *

Abbas ambled along the frosted campus lawn as the late afternoon sun twinkled against the windscreens of cars in the distance. His pocket vibrated. He continued walking for a moment, his plan of disposing of his phone for good by the morning keeping him unphased. He checked it casually.

@introversial
Replying to @MCMongrel
Just so everyone knows, he made all this up for clout. He just told me.

Abbas sunk as the numbers soared. By morning the Tweet would surpass 200 likes and 100 retweets, and

Maryam's bantering ad-lib piggybacking off the replies would earn her 36 new followers.

(grit)

AIDAN MARTIN
Groomed

I stood outside of that McDonalds with my heart racing. It was a dark winter evening and I could feel the cold air sharply stinging my cheeks. Lying to my Mum about who I was meeting didn't feel great. What was I supposed to do though? I could hardly tell her I was actually here to meet a man I had been talking to on the Internet instead of the 'friends' I was allegedly meeting. I was only fifteen. Still in school. As she drove off, I felt a horrible sense of having betrayed her. Writing this now I feel it was an even greater betrayal to my younger self. I was already on the way to ending my childhood innocence and yet I had no idea of the impact those moments would have on my entire life.

Ruminating now as an addict in recovery from substance abuse and sexual addiction, I have the gift of hindsight. Through recovery, education, therapy and life experience I can better analyse exactly *how* I became a schoolboy waiting for this older man to drive all the way up to Livingston, Scotland, from England to meet me. At the time, however, I had no clue. I still thought shouting out the words "cheese and ham" as the teachers read out pupils' names from the class register was utterly hilarious, as did my group of friends. I was also suicidal and vulnerable, often thinking of ways to end my life or fantasising about being somewhere else, anywhere else, completely out of my own head.

Checking my pay-as-you-go mobile phone, which I had funded through my paper round, I knew *he* was on his way, almost near. My imagination ran wild wondering what he looked like and exactly what was going to happen once we met. We had never seen each other, never sent pictures or spoken on webcam. We had only chatted online or on the phone. Our conversations took place in chat rooms mostly. At that time all I knew was that he was supportive, and he understood me. He always sounded cheery on the phone and his Northern English accent made me trust him all the more. My mother, aunties and uncles all had Manchester or 'Manc' accents from growing up in Salford. So when Derek spoke in that Northern twang, I believed that he was warm and humorous too.

More than anything else, I was just happy to be in the world of fantasy, out of my reality as a struggling-to-cope, suicidal teenage boy. Already, at such a young age, my ever-growing addictions were taking hold of me and my mental health, but much like this rapidly approaching encounter with *him*, I had no grasp of the enormity of it. Nowhere near.

Pacing back and forward, teeth chattering, I kept my eyes peeled for a white van. That was all I had to go on. He told me he owned a textile company and that his work took him to West Lothian, where I lived. Livingston, West Lothian. Oddly enough, I recall this being one of the first conversations we ever had. Where we both lived. As an immature young boy, I had no reason to think any more of it or to question it.

With every passing van my heart smashed against my chest a little harder. Thoughts invaded my consciousness in frenetic fashion. Nerves truly had me now. What would he look like? I knew what I looked like. Skinny, blonde hair, blue eyes, freckles and tall with slightly protruding teeth that I hadn't quite grown into. I wore black nylon tracksuit bottoms, trainers and a sports hoody, much like many other gangly teenage boys of my generation in the early 'noughties'.

I wouldn't have to wonder what he looked like for much longer. An ordinary looking white work van pulled slowly into the McDonalds car park. Headlights blinded my eyes as the warmth of my accelerated breathing mixed with the ice-cold air. Once the lights dimmed I got a glimpse of the man at the steering wheel peering back at me, and it took me by surprise.

Derek waved me over to the van, and now that this was a reality my adolescent mind raced and my body began to pulsate with a blend of adrenaline, fear and nerves. He looked old and chubby, like someone's grandad. Those were the thoughts in my mind. I began to question everything. "What am I doing here? Should I run away? *Can* I run away? I'm not gay so *why* am I here meeting this older man?" I kept thinking, "He's driven all this way so surely I *have* to meet him?" No longer was I in the safety of fantasy, sitting behind a computer screen in my dad's study with a keyboard or in my bedroom on my brick-like mobile phone, where at any moment I could press the red 'end call' button and escape. Here I was, very much in a real situation, frozen on the spot and faced with danger. Then without thought, like an out-of-body experience as if watching myself from afar, I walked towards his van.

Falsely and naively I told myself that simply getting in the van wouldn't mean anything and I could get out of this whenever I wanted. This warped thinking would contribute to many years of compulsive behaviour in my life still to come as I would be gripped in the brutal world of substance and sexual addiction. As for right there in that moment, this ruling thought of 'act now, think later' took me into Derek's van where I got a better look at the man I had been speaking to since I was fourteen, almost a year leading up to this furtive meeting.

"Hi Aidan!" he said in a booming Northern accent as I sat down in the passenger seat, acutely aware that he centrally locked the doors. Waves of claustrophobia and panic engulfed me. "What happens now?" I thought. For the first time in my life, that Northern accent, usually a nostalgic expression of love, humour and safety, was causing distress and alarm. And just like that, we drove off. My senses were in overdrive. The sound of the van's handbrake creaking, peddles being pressed and the ticking of the indicators roared in my brain. It didn't just feel like we were driving away from McDonalds. I felt like I was being driven away from safety. I was in a world of the unknown now. A terrifying place to be.

Derek didn't look or behave like someone to be terrified of in any particular way. His glasses magnified his eyes. I was aware of his rogue eyebrow hairs sticking out in places. He smelled of coffee and had slightly olive skin tinged by age. His hands were small but thick. He had dark hair, greying in places with a tanned bald spot at the back. I noticed he wore a hi-vis vest over his white shirt, which his stomach swelled from. He had black trousers on. What creeped me out instantly was his smile. It was crooked. As though half of his face didn't want to conform.

Despite this no longer being fantasy, it wasn't reality for me either. I didn't feel like I was actually there. It was as though I was in a hypnotic trance, which may sound cliché, but it is the only way I can relay this truthfully. As we drove off, Derek spoke to me about how long the drive was and how busy he was with work. Everything felt so strange. So unreal. So numb. Seeing that I wasn't saying very much, I remember Derek pointing out how shy I was compared to how outgoing I had been in conversation online. It was true. We had spoken of all sorts online.

Regularly I had told Derek how suicidal I was. He would listen. I would tell him how I was struggling at school and how hard my dad was on me. Derek would take my side. Being a young lad who never knew his biological father and struggled with a strict stepfather (who I call my dad), it felt amazing to have someone who understood me.

One night, as I sat in my dad's study talking to Derek online, I was at breaking point. Crying hysterically, I told him I wanted to end my life. With tears splashing down onto the keyboard, I confided in Derek that I was crying. He told me he was crying too. It made me feel like we were connected.

I shared some of my other serious problems with Derek too. Like the day my father stormed into my bedroom and threw down a £500 phone bill in disgust. He was furious with me. In shock I hadn't realised I had run up such a massive bill. Oblivious at this stage in my life, my sexual addiction was already destroying my mind and soul. I had stolen porn magazines from our local shop in which I worked as a paper boy. It was easy to steal porn magazines and VHS pornography tapes as I gathered the papers needed for my round each morning before school. In these magazines were phone numbers. Unbeknown to me they were premium rate.

One day I phoned one of the numbers, which had been described as phoning a dominatrix. I was drawn to phoning this number to experience degradation. I felt like a drunk sitting on the pub steps before opening time. I couldn't resist. Still far too young to understand why I sought out such self-harming treatment, that first phone call led to many, many more. Phoning those numbers gave me a rush I can only compare to a heroin addict's first hit. Complete ecstasy, escapism and carnal pleasure in one easy phone call. I didn't even need to do or say anything, it was all automated, like listening to a story. Easy for a teenager to get away with without any age verification needed.

Looking back now, the content of those automated messages was cheesy compared to the hardcore porn I had been accustomed to since I was ten years old. "Get down on your knees you snivelling little worm… lick my boots clean" or "I am wearing shiny, black, leather thigh-high boots with nine-inch heels for you to suck! ...get down and worship them" and the likes, always in an older woman's English accent.

Lacking self-awareness, I was experiencing the escalation of the disease of addiction. Without realising it, another habit or 'ritual' had begun. Every chance I got I was phoning, sneaking into my dad's study to pick up the phone and call the number. Once I had listened to a story once or twice it lacked the same impact and didn't do anything for me anymore, so I explored the plethora of numbers offered from the range of magazines I had been stealing and collecting.

Such calls now would arouse nothing more in me than laughter at how tame and ridiculous it sounds, however, I was desperate for interaction. The phone lines had been a buzz, but once I discovered chat rooms it was a game changer. It felt like an upgrade. I still got a good hit from the phone calls, but I couldn't go back to just listening to automated messages. I had become addicted to talking to real people. Or what I believed were real people. And anyway, I was about to be caught out for my secret phone calls.

When Dad found out, it was one of my first experiences of the consequences of addiction. My automated phone calling habit came to a halt the day British Telecom sent my dad the bill and he phoned the numbers himself. That was a type of shame and degradation I certainly didn't enjoy. Cringe and embarrassment too, especially when my very straight-laced, Catholic father brought me to task. Feeling exposed like that wounded me with feelings of guilt that I didn't know how to handle.

Luckily, Derek was there. He placated me as I ranted about how hard my dad was on me. Pandering to my young desires, I distinctly remember Derek supporting and justifying my behaviour. Yet again, he understood me.

Perhaps this opened the door to discussing sexual fantasies with each other. I can't quite recall the first time that happened. But it did.

During conversation I even indignantly expressed to Derek my anger at my father telling me I would be paying the bill every week from my £15-per-week paper round earnings and my £10-a-week pocket money. This was a hammer blow at a time when I had recently discovered the joy of straight vodka and whiskey, purchased from a schoolmate each week who stole it out of his father's small, family-run shop. Part of the reason I told Derek this was to hint for some money to help me pay my father. Derek was unable to help me pay it, he claimed, but he did want to buy me a new watch.

Fast forward to the moment in hand and here we were, in his van, talking in person. Or should I say Derek was talking and I was listening. Almost laughing, he said words to me I will never forget for as long as I live. He repeated these particular words a few times: "You look like a scared rabbit in the headlights," as though we were on our way to a theme park to ride a scary rollercoaster for the first time. In truth we were on our way somewhere far scarier. We were driving to a local hotel where I would present as Derek's nephew, carefully coached as to what I should say in the unlikely event of anyone questioning why our accents didn't match up. He had even gone to the effort of specifically asking for two separate beds to make this clandestine meeting seem all the more innocent.

Standing in front of the receptionist I was on high alert and the things capturing my attention seem strange to me even now. For example, I was extremely aware of how squishy the carpet felt under my feet or how there were framed pictures on walls looking lost against a backdrop of long white corridors. It was a woman on reception, yet I cannot recall her face or any of her features. What I do remember, is that Derek had to write both of our names down. He gave me his surname. That was the most surreal thing of all, to see my first name followed with this stranger's surname, my online friend who felt different to me now that I was standing next to him pretending to be his nephew.

Nonchalantly, Derek chatted away to the receptionist about how he was up in Scotland seeing family and working. Clearly at ease with this process of lying, it felt like a pre-emptive strike. Truth be told I wanted them to talk for hours. I needed time. I wanted to run away but it felt far too late for that. Regrettably, just like my porn habit, things continued escalating and once all the formalities were completed the receptionist handed Derek a key with a cheap looking plastic fob containing a door number. We wouldn't have to walk far. The room was on the same floor we were on.

Leading the way, Derek swung the keys around in his thick hands and was even whistling. Acting so normal yet with such incongruity felt like such a paradox. Hearing the key fob open the door sent shockwaves right through me. Fear gripped me. With each step, I walked closer to the end of my childhood. Trembling, I timorously followed Derek into the room. He closed the door behind him and repeated those awful words, forever etched in my brain: "What's the matter Aidan? You look like a scared rabbit in the headlights. I'm not gonna hurt you." I was already hurting. I was scared. I wanted to go home and get a hot cup of tea and watch movies in my bed, in the safety of my home, my parents in their room and my wee brother across the hall in his room.

Telling me to sit down, Derek began to remove his outer clothing, hi-vis vest, boots, belt and so on. I sat down on the edge of the double bed, noticing a single bed made up near the window. I was, of course, there as his nephew, so that single bed was supposed to be mine. Yet again I became aware of silly things. The small kettle and cups with little biscuits on offer beside the tea and coffee. A small remote control on the bedside table for the television. I could see glimpses of the car park through the curtains that Derek went over to close.

Derek turned to look at me. He stared for a long time. It felt like a lifetime to me. He was sweating and breathing heavily. From the look on his face and the prolonged silence it seemed like he was disappointed at how shy I was. He set up a laptop as he spoke to me, repeating how scared I looked. As he stood up I noticed something I hadn't previously. He was short. Shorter than me. It feels funny to say but he reminded me of a gnome without the beard. This really hit me hard in that moment. I really didn't know anything about this man at all, did I? Online you build up an image of someone, the image they give you and your mind fills in the blanks with qualities you would like them to have. I had been searching for something in those chatrooms, or someone, and I *did* discuss sexual fantasies, but I was the child and I was vulnerable.

To put me at ease, Derek suggested I relax as he went for a shower. But not before he presented me with two gifts. One was in a box and I opened it to see a brand-new waterproof, digital sports watch. It was black and red. Derek seemed so chuffed to give it to me whilst I felt confused over exactly how to feel, but I made sure to thank him. Finally, before going for his shower he pulled from a plastic carrier bag a bottle of Buckfast. I found this to be truly astonishing. If that moment hadn't felt so serious, I would have found the idea completely hilarious that this older English man would have walked into a corner shop and purchased a bottle of Buckfast. To me, only young Scottish lads and girls drank this to get smashed out in the streets on a Friday night having all lied to our parents about our whereabouts. It reminded me of some of the lads in school I had difficulties with. It reminded me of the violent streets I grew up and hung out in. It reminded me my biological father never wanted me. Buckfast epitomised my working-class upbringing at a time in my life of painful suicidal thoughts and rebellious teenage behaviour. Yet here I was, in my apparent fantasy world, sitting on the edge of a double bed with a bottle of it in my hand as Derek went for a shower.

Twisting the top of the bottle, I swiftly removed the lid and knocked my head back to gulp down that cough syrup-like sweetness of this tonic wine. That familiar rush followed as it raced around my body. I genuinely loved that feeling every time I guzzled down Buckfast. It felt like leaving my consciousness behind and becoming someone else. This time was different though. I clung to the edge of that bed as though I was hanging from a dangerous cliff. Making my way through the bottle, I listened to the water ebbing away then the sound of a shower curtain swishing back.

Anxiously I waited, rooted to the spot on that double bed. Derek walked into the room and stood before me with water still running down his body and a white towel wrapped around his waist, failing to disguise how excited he was. It's curious the things you remember about an abuser. That bald patch on his head, the wry smile and swollen belly. His horrible overgrown toenails with a mole on one of his big toes. The fading arm tattoos. Which of all his characteristics, broke my heart the most. They reminded me of my grandad, who also had fading arm tattoos. My grandad made me feel so loved and having his tattooed arms around me were always a feeling of protection, love, safety and acceptance. To see this man in front of me with tattoos much the same, damaged me in ways that would take years to understand.

Before anything happened, Derek pulled out one more surprise. A porn mag, his mobile phone and some premium rate numbers. Drunk as I was becoming, and grateful for the gift of the watch, I felt like I owed it to my friend to not let him down. I lay back on the double bed with my head resting on enormous soft pillows. Derek dialled a number on his phone and gave it to me. I placed the phone to my ear and listened to the familiar automated voice as I kept swigging the Buckfast to get the familiar rush of alcohol. Amongst all those familiar pleasures, what Derek did to me next was the most unfamiliar, horrific experience for a teenage boy who liked girls and was still a virgin.

I closed my eyes as Derek undressed me and performed a sex act on me. Never in my life had a man or even another male touched me in such a way before. I wasn't homophobic, far from it. I just wasn't gay and if this had been with an adult woman, I wouldn't have been ready either. Not mentally or emotionally, if even physically. What Derek was doing to me felt alien and it felt wrong. I knew in my gut it was all wrong. I just lay there and hoped it would be over quick.

Something else was happening that I had never experienced before either. Suddenly the automated phone lines weren't working for me. To be blunt, I couldn't get an erection or get aroused. This frustrated Derek. I have to clarify that he was never hostile, ever. It always felt like I was letting down a friend and so I tried my best to keep going with it. Even the alcohol wasn't making me feel as invincible as it usually did. Finally giving up on that particular sex act, Derek changed positions and lay on top of me.

All I remember from this was his weight on top of me, looking up at him and seeing his face. It was expressionless. I was mentally gone from this moment onwards. I just wasn't there anymore. The automated phone voice now sounded like a continuous drone and I didn't move a muscle. I just waited for it to be over. Numb. Detached. Anesthetized from alcohol and shock. Eventually it was over and he rolled off me, handing me his wet, white towel to clean myself up as he returned to the bathroom to do the same.

Then he came back with a big smile on his face that reminded me of the cheery man from the phone calls we used to have. Like a shapeshifter he got himself dressed, as I did too, and approached me with a big, warm hug. It felt like overcoming some kind of massive experience, as if I had survived a serious operation at hospital or something.

Before he dropped me back to that McDonalds and back to my life, forever changed, he sat next to me on the bed and just spoke. He told me his son had died some years before and how much it broke his heart. He spoke about his wife and his other children. He even, for some reason, told me he had a side job performing pop-up discos at weddings and that at certain times of the year he made an adequate wage from it. Like I mentioned before, it is a curious thing, the particulars you remember.

How do you go back to your so-called normal life after this? Feeling worthless inside is what had already sent me down this path of self-destruction. After meeting Derek, my sense of relationships and intimacy was corrupted and my identity over my sexuality confused.

Little could I have known, there was still worse to come in my life. I do not pinpoint this moment as defining my addictions. I was already on my way to becoming a full blown sexual and substances dual-addict. But it certainly sped up the process and provided me with trauma that would take years to understand and overcome. I still had many horrendous battles ahead. What I could never have imagined at that point of life, was that there would also be experiences beyond my wildest dreams in my future. Most importantly, I would go on a journey in which a *Higher Power* would guide my life in ways beyond human understanding, including the discovery of Derek's true identity.

* * *

'Groomed' is Chapter 1 of *Euphoric Recall,* Aidan Martin's debut memoir. It is a raw and honest tale about addiction, recovery and growing up on the rough streets of Livingston. To be released on 12 February 2021 by Guts Publishing.

(happy-ish ending)

RADOSLAV ROCHALLYI

Desperate leprosy

$$I\ thank\ you^x = for + \frac{everything}{I\ am!} + \frac{strength\ to\ be^{\,2}}{alone!} +$$

$$+ \frac{time\ is^3}{running\ out!} + \cdots, \, -\infty < for\ the\ us < \infty$$

CONTRIBUTORS

Ross Baxter – 'Self Service'
After thirty years at sea, Ross Baxter now concentrates on writing sci-fi and horror fiction. His varied work has been published in print by numerous publishing houses in US and UK short-story anthologies. He has won a number of awards, including the Horror Novel Review.Com best creation short fiction prize. Married to a Norwegian and with two Anglo-Viking kids, he now lives in Derby, England.

Julian Bishop – 'Tracker'
Julian Bishop is a former television journalist living in North London who is a member of the collective group Poets For The Planet. A former runner-up in the Ginkgo Prize for Eco Poetry, he's one of four prize-winning poets featured in a 2020 pamphlet called *Poems For The Planet*. He's also been shortlisted for the Bridport Poetry Prize.

Piotr Bockowski – 'a sister of her sister. (No… it can't be her!)'
Piotr Bockowski is a philosopher of biotech, body performer & video artist, working between Hong Kong & London for over a decade. Since 2015 he has been curating Chronic Illness performance art events at his squatted microbes-contaminated space The Dungeons of Polymorphous Pan in London, at the same time researching Fungi Media and teaching Media Art at Goldsmiths, University of London. Piotr writes for academic and online journals as well as publishes with art, subcultural & fetish zines in London. In 2019 he launched Peach Spore Press

with Gabriella Gasparini, a platform focused on body philosophy.

Andrew M Bowen – 'E-Romance'
Andrew M Bowen has published about 105 poems and is seeking to publish two novels. He is also an actor who has appeared in ten independent films, eight stage productions, two radio teleplays, and two podcasts.

Kes Brookland – 'Document Recovery'
Kes Brookland is a writer and political scientist who came from the middle of nowhere, and so can't really complain about being somewhere. Their work, which has previously been published in *Riggwelter Magazine*, is concerned with digital spaces, the darker corners of interiority, and the end of the world. The first two make for far better research objects, but all three make for excellent poetry.

Erica Buist – 'To All the Avatars I've Loved Before'
Erica Buist is a journalist, lecturer, and author. Formerly a staffer at the *Guardian*, her writing has also been published in the *Sunday Times*, the *BBC*, *Medium*, various literary magazines and performed at live storytelling events. She has been a writer-in-residence at the Wellstone Center in the Redwoods, Vermont Studio Center, Faber, Virginia Center for the Creative Arts and Arte Studio Ginestrelle. Erica regularly appears on BBC Radio, and her first book—a hybrid of nonfiction and memoir called *This Party's Dead*—will be published in 2021 by Unbound. She speaks five languages, mostly to her dog.

Roger Craik – 'In the Machine (2004)'
Roger Craik was born in Leicester and has worked in universities in Turkey, Romania, Bulgaria and America. He has written four full-length books of poetry, of which the

latest is *Down Stranger Roads* (Blazevox, 2014). He lives in Ashtabula, Ohio.

Ugochukwu Damian – 'Survival'
Ugochukwu Damian, Nigerian writer & Poet, is the 1st runner up in the Nigerian Students Poetry Prize 2019. He was one of the 21 mentees in the second cohort of the SLM Mentorship Programme and an alumnus of the Purple Hibiscus Trust Creative Writing Workshop. His works have appeared/forthcoming in *African Writer*, The Rising Phoenix Press, *Barren Magazine*, *The Penn Review*, and elsewhere. He is currently interning as the Contributing Interviewer for *Poetry at Africa in Dialogue*.

Rab Ferguson – 'The Call'
Rab Ferguson is a York based writer of fiction and poetry. His short stories can be found in *Storgy*, *Litro*, *Under the Fable*, *Unsung Stories*, *Beyond the Walls* and *VoiceIn Journal*. He's also a performing storyteller, and has been known to wear a woollen cape. He likes cycling, cats, and Bruce Springsteen, but has not yet found a practical way to combine those interests.

Liam Hogan – 'Plastic People'
Liam Hogan is an award-winning short story writer, with stories in *Best of British Science Fiction 2016*, and *Best of British Fantasy 2018* (NewCon Press). He's been published by *Analog*, *Daily Science Fiction*, and Flametree Press, among others. He helps host Liars' League London, volunteers at the creative writing charity Ministry of Stories, and lives and avoids work in London.

Lydia Hounat – 'closure, decoded' and 'Today is a good day to be alive.'

Lydia Hounat is a British-Algerian writer and photographer. Her work has appeared in *HOBART*, *Peach Magazine*, *Spontaneous Poetics*, and has work forthcoming in *Copy: A Magazine of Recycled Materials from Wasted Books*. She critiques contemporary literature at *LITBITCH*, edits interdisciplinary art zine, *SOBER*. and was recently a Poet-in-Residence with Manchester Metropolitan University's Special Collections Archives and First Draft Cabaret. She lives in Cornwall.

Julianne Ingles – 'Dante's Dream'

A Chicago native, Julianne Ingles is a writer, editor and founder of Guts Publishing. Her degrees include an MA in Creative Writing and an MA in Modern Literature, both from Goldsmiths, University of London. Her websites are inglesart.com and gutspublishing.com. She lives in London.

Lydia Luke – 'copper & lead'

Lydia Luke is a poet and writer based in Epsom, UK. Her work has been published by *AFROPUNK*, *Syla Studio*, *Kandaka*, *Sweet-Thang Zine*, *Lungs Project* and *Lacuna Lit*. Her writing practice predicates on delineating the human condition thru the prisms of Black womanhood, sensuality, music, the sacred and radical honesty. She co-facilitates PRISM WRITERS; a writer's group for Black women held at the Southbank Centre and has a master's degree in Black British Writing from Goldsmiths, University of London.

Q.M. – 'I Should Have Loved My Babe'

Q.M. is from China and currently lives in Edinburgh. His poems have appeared in *Constellations*, *Lucky Jefferson*, *The Holiday Café*, *Scribendi*, and *Blue Tiger Review*, among others.

Tamara MacLeod —
'Cyberwhores_Sex_Robots_and_Aliens'
Tamara MacLeod is the pseudonym of a freelance writer, sex worker and activist based in England. Her words can be found online at *Aeon Magazine* and *3:AM Magazine*. Follow her on Twitter @HiTamaraMacLeod. She invites hate mail directly to hitamaramacleod@gmail.com. For anything else, cast a circle with five black candles and say her name three times.

Aidan Martin – 'Groomed'
Aidan Martin is a debuting memoirist. His first book discusses his recovery from addiction and many traumas including sexual abuse. Aidan is a fiancé to his beautiful partner and a proud father of two beautiful children. He currently works as a mental health and addictions worker as well as studying social work at master's degree level. In 2017 he gained an honours degree in Social Sciences: with Criminology and Sociology. As a grateful recovering addict, Aidan is heavily involved in the recovery scene. He is currently working on a Scottish working-class fiction around trance culture.

Drew Pisarra – 'Actinium'
Drew Pisarra is the author of *Publick Spanking* (1996), a collection of short stories published by Future Tense, and *Infinity Standing Up* (2019), a collection of queer sonnets published by Capturing Fire. He is also one half of Saint Flashlight, an ongoing literary activation project with Molly Gross that finds inventive ways to get poetry into public spaces.

Asad Raja – 'Home / Screen'
Asad Raja is a British Pakistani, born and raised in South London. He is currently studying Mechanical Engineering

at Imperial College London. He has been writing as a hobby since high school, producing a stage-play script, 'Rhineland Bastards', that was longlisted in a National Theatre competition. 'Home / Screen' is his first short story, which he wrote as part of an elective creative writing module at university. He has since written a second short story, 'He Made Them Forget Themselves'. Asad is also the Music Editor for his university newspaper, *Felix*, and the Founder and President of Imperial's Hip Hop Society.

Radoslav Rochallyi – 'Biological mimicry' and 'Desperate leprosy'
Rochallyi was born in Bardejov, today the Slovak Republic. The author finished his studies in Philosophy at the Faculty of Arts of the UNIPO and completed postgraduate Ph.D. studies. Rochallyi is the author of eleven books. He writes in Slovak, English, and German. He debuted with the collection of poetry *Panoptikum: Haikai no renga* (2004), written in Japanese haiku. Rochallyi has a close relationship to mathematics and philosophy.

Ellie Stewart – 'Send Nudes'
Ellie Stewart is currently studying for an MA in Creative and Life Writing at Goldsmiths, University of London. She previously worked in fundraising and communications in the charity sector. Her non-fiction, poetry and short stories have been published in various places online and in print including *Goldfish Anthology*, *Her Stry* and *Popshot Quarterly* – you can find out more at www.alittlefantastic.com. She lives in London and is working on writing her memoir.

Calum Walker – 'Purpose'
Calum Walker is a freelance short story writer and a recent graduate of a Creative Writing MA course, courtesy of

University of Brighton. He has had a lifelong fascination with the crossroads where the farcical and the macabre intersect, and as such feels most at home when writing horror, comedy, weird fiction, or any given combination of the three.

Greg Wilder – 'I'd Give Her the Dickinson'
Greg Wilder (also known by the stage name Slay! the Dragon) is an award-winning writer, full-time student, and spoken word performer, currently residing in Schenectady, NY. After a long, downhill battle with alcohol and drug addiction, Greg entered treatment in June of 2017 and rediscovered the therapeutic potential of art and writing. Today, with over 3 years clean, Greg shares the healing power of poetry with other recovering addicts as an intern for a drug and alcohol treatment center. Greg studies Human Services and English at SUNY Schenectady.

Kristan X – 'Metrics'
Kristan X is a writer, sex nerd and the (somewhat twisted) mind behind the professionally-filthy sex blog Lascivity [http://www.lascivity.co.uk/]. He's based in Edinburgh, but travels extensively. He reads a lot. He's obsessed with psychology, sociology, games of all kind, true crime and tech.

COPYRIGHTS FOR INDIVIDUAL TITLES

ABOUT GUTS PUBLISHING

We are an independent publisher in London. The name came from the obvious—it takes guts to publish just about anything. We are the home to the freaks and misfits of the literary world.

We like uncomfortable topics. Our tagline: Ballsy books about life.

Our debut anthology, *Stories About Penises* (Nov 2019), is a collection of fiction, nonfiction and poetry about, exactly what it sounds like. To quote a prominent Australian author, 'Quite possibly the best title of the year.' We think so too.

Our third anthology is *Sending Nudes* (publishing 2021).

Our debut memoir, *Euphoric Recall* by Aidan Martin, will be released 12 February 2021. A raw, honest tale about addiction, recovery and growing up on the rough streets of Livingston, Scotland. Aidan's childhood friend, Mark Deans, created the illustration for the cover. Aidan's website is: http://aidanmartinauthor.co.uk

To order our books visit: www.gutspublishing.com/books. We are happy to sign your books, just send an email after you place your order: gutspublishing@gmail.com

Thank you for reading, and thank you for your support!